LEGAL AND
POLITICAL ISSUES
IN SPECIAL EDUCATION

LEGAL AND POLITICAL ISSUES IN SPECIAL EDUCATION

By

JAMES J. CREMINS, Ph.D.

*Associate Professor of Special Education
and Rehabilitation
Boston College
Chestnut Hill, Massachusetts*

CHARLES C THOMAS • PUBLISHER
Springfield • Illinois • U.S.A.

Published and Distributed Throughout the World by

CHARLES C THOMAS • PUBLISHER

2600 South First Street

Springfield, Illinois 62717

© *1983 by* CHARLES C THOMAS • PUBLISHER

ISBN 0-398-04878-9

Library of Congress Catalog Card Number: 83-4841

With THOMAS BOOKS *careful attention is given to all details of manufacturing and
design. It is the Publisher's desire to present books that are satisfactory as to their physical
qualities and artistic possibilities and appropriate for their particular use.* THOMAS
BOOKS *will be true to those laws of quality that assure a good name and good will.*

Printed in the United States of America
Q-R-3

Library of Congress Cataloging in Publication Data

Cremins, James J.
    Legal and political issues in special education

    Bibliography: p.
    1. Handicapped children--Education--Law and legisla-
tion--United States. 2. Handicapped children--Educa-
tion--Government policy--United States.   I. Title.
KF4210.C73   1983   344.73'0791   83-4841
ISBN 0-398-04878-9   347.304791

This book is dedicated to Jim and Mary Cremins,
my first teachers.

PREFACE

THE field of special education is in a period of transition. Retrenchment, not advancement, seems to be characteristic today of education for the handicapped. Advancement and progress characteristic of the last ten years seems to be giving way to rethinking and re-examining goals of education for the handicapped. Serious questions are being raised about the role of the federal government in this process and whether the "right to education" for the handicapped requires maximizing each individual's potential or merely providing access to services.

Currently, a number of important issues have surfaced and the resolution of these issues will have a significant impact on the future of special education. These issues include:

- The continuing debate over amendments to P.L. 94-142, which would remove the IEP requirement, severely limit parental participation in the special education process, curtail related services, and would also eliminate the appeals process.
- The proposal by the Office of Education to deregulate Section 504.
- The significance of the *Rowley* case. This is the first case in which the United States Supreme Court has interpreted the intent of P.L. 94-142.
- The continuing effort by the Reagan administration to cut funding for education and human service programs.

In order to protect and preserve the rights of handicapped children to a free, appropriate public education, parents, professionals, and advocates must clearly understand the substance and implications of these legal and political issues. Such issues are the concern of this book.

Legal and Political Issues in Special Education is designed to provide an overview of current legal and political issues in special education for teachers, parents, advocates, and other professionals concerned with the education of handicapped children.

The book is divided into seven chapters, each dealing with a specific topic. The first chapter provides an introduction to the evolution of special education as a discipline and also traces the increasing role of the federal government in providing education for the handicapped. The second chapter presents a comparison of P.L. 94-142, Section 504 (P.L. 93-112) and Massachusetts special education law Chapter 766. Chapter Three focuses on problems associated with the use of minimum competency tests with handicapped students. Chapter Four examines the issue of extended school year for the handicapped. Chapter Five deals with the area of suspension and expulsion of handicapped students. Chapter Six describes the increasing need for parents to serve as advocates for their handicapped children as the courts take a less active role and appeals hearings assume more importance. Chapter Seven provides the reader with a summary of selected important cases that will and are having a significant impact on the education of handicapped children.

J.J.C.

ACKNOWLEDGMENTS

Many persons, present and past, have contributed to the development of this book. In particular, my teachers, A.J. Pappanikou, Melvin Reich, Michael Turvey, and L.J. Stoppleworth; my students, especially Robert Sherman and Alice Slattery; and, above all, my wife Lorraine, and my children, Jay and Colby. Their love and support make all things possible.

CONTENTS

LEGAL AND
POLITICAL ISSUES
IN SPECIAL EDUCATION

CHAPTER 1

SPECIAL EDUCATION: FROM EVOLUTION TO REVOLUTION

Introduction

THROUGHOUT history man has had difficulty dealing with people who are different. Different may mean minority group members, the elderly, the poor, the criminal, but especially the handicapped. Societal treatment of handicapped citizens has evolved through three distinct stages. First, the handicapped were abused and neglected. They were subjected to exposure in ancient Greece, abandoned by the Romans and ridiculed as fools and jesters during the Middle Ages. Second, the handicapped were segregated and placed in secluded institutions far from the mainstream of society. Third, over the last hundred years there has been a painfully slow process of integration and participation for the handicapped.

Recently, the future has been bright for the handicapped. Their civil rights are now guaranteed by the Rehabilitation Act of 1973 (P.L. 93-112, Sec. 504). Furthermore, the right of every handicapped child to a free, appropriate public education is now mandated by P.L. 94-142.

The purpose of this chapter is to identify the major factors that contributed to the current plethora of educational services for handicapped children. These factors include (1) the evolution of special education as a discipline, (2) the increasing role of the federal government in education from the late 1800s to the present day, and

(3) the tremendous increase in court cases dealing with education of handicapped children during the seventies.

In addition to the factors mentioned above, many other important issues could be included in this analysis. For example, the contribution of pioneers like Dix, Kirk, Cruickshank, Itard, Seguin, Montessori and many others has been profound; likewise, the development of the Council for Exceptional Children has been a major positive force. The movement to organize parents of handicapped children was also a significant catalyst for change. The list goes on. However, a discussion of these issues is beyond the scope of this chapter, which will attempt to give the reader a brief overview of the field of special education with emphasis on issues related to laws and court cases.

EVOLUTION

Brief History of Special Education

According to Heiny, available histories in English trace the beginning of special education first to the Middle East, then to the Mediterranean under Christianity, next to Europe, and finally to the United States.

The term *special education* was first used in Germany about 1863. The history of special education began with the recognition that differences within and between individuals existed to such an extent that variations in treatment were appropriate for dealing with those called different. The idea of special education surely reflected a humanistic concern for less-fortunate citizens and recognition of man's responsibility to his handicapped brothers and sisters.

The earliest general use of special education was provided for those who were deaf and blind.

Fundamental to the development of special services is the dawn of the age of humanism in Europe during the eighteenth century. 'The education of the deaf and blind in France at this time is an important milestone,' reported Eugene Doll. 'In looking at the training of the deaf, I see the first emergence of special education. The key name here is Jacob Rodriguez Periere. He astonished everyone by teaching the deaf to speak' (Heiny, 1971).

For centuries the handicapped were considered to be useless, non-productive members of society. Co..sequently, they were abused, ignored, and ridiculed. However, early in the nineteenth century it was discovered that they could be trained. This discovery led to the establishment of numerous training schools or asylums. This training concept emigrated from Europe to the United States, and, in 1817, Reverend Thomas Gallaudet established the first residential school in America, called the Asylum for the Deaf, in Hartford, Connecticut. In the 1820s, the first training school for the blind opened, and, by the middle of the century, Samuel Gridley Howe had established the Institution for Idiotic Children in Massachusetts. Although the term had not yet been invented, these early teachers of the deaf and blind were surely *special educators*.

The Industrial Revolution, late in the eighteenth century, caused a great migration of people from rural to urban areas. This great social upheaval led to the establishment of standardized institutions for various types of handicapped people. Interestingly, labeling the handicapped served to legitimize the provision of differential legal, medical, residential, economic, and socialization care. Labeling was, in fact, a key to more efficient use of resources and care for the handicapped. However, in general, the promise of the early nineteenth century gave way to disappointment in the mid and late nineteenth century. This period was characterized by public and professional apathy towards problems of the handicapped. Institutions thrived, but the promise of a shift from training and isolation to education and integration did not occur. The goal of society was to train the handicapped to function in the institution rather than educating them to function in society. Some reasons for society's general attitude of neglect during this time may include the following:

1. The handicapped were ignored while America was caught up in its Industrial Revolution.
2. Few people had the training, interest, or motivation to work with the handicapped.
3. The handicapped were hidden away in secluded institutions and were forgotten about.
4. Society preferred to hide its mistakes.

In 1898, Alexander Graham Bell, speaking before the National

Education Association, pointed out that handicapped children had a right to education through the public schools. It would be eighty years before Bell's plea would become mandated by law.

The beginning of the twentieth century saw progress in special education occur as part of the general movement in public health (Shaw & Lucas, 1970). The First World War and its residue of handicapped soldiers in need of rehabilitation gave further impetus to the special education movement. Furthermore, day-school programs, which allowed handicapped children to live at home, were developing early in the twentieth century. Finally, the advent of intelligence testing and the resulting classification of retarded children into specific categories based on scores led to the establishment of schools and programs for the mentally retarded.

At the local level, special education began with assignment of teachers to work in special classes. The city of Providence offered special classes for the retarded as early as 1895. Boston, Springfield, and Chicago started before 1900, and Los Angeles and Philadelphia followed shortly. The earliest special education classes were for the mildiy retarded. Between 1900 and 1910, the New York City Board of Education established ungraded classes, which were known later as classes for children with retarded mental development.

Programs and facilities for handicapped children increased rapidly during the early part of this century. Some reasons for this increase include continued migration from rural to urban areas and the tremendous influx of foreign immigrants to the United States. America, in the midst of tremendous industrial expansion during the early part of this century, desperately needed workers. Consequently, immigrants poured in from throughout the world. Most of these people came to America with a language and culture that was foreign and strange. The so-called "melting pot" theory never worked for many of these people. They were often rejected, ignored, and isolated by society.

The children of these immigrants had little chance to succeed. They were handicapped by their language, customs, and the color of their skin. They had little educational opportunity, poor nutrition, and inadequate health care. All these factors added to the increasing number of handicapped children during this period of history. As the number of programs and facilities for the handicapped increased, so did the need for qualified teachers. To meet this need, Charles S. Berry established the first teacher-training program for special educators at the Lapeer State Home and Training School in Michigan in 1914. Shortly thereafter, Charles M. Elliot established the first college program in special education at Michigan State Normal College. Elliot's efforts resulted in establishment of the Rackman School of Special Education at Eastern Michigan. For many years, Rackman was the chief source of special educators for the United States.

Prior to the Second World War, significant progress was made in developing strategies and techniques for teaching retarded children. The actual number of special programs and educators was, however, smaller than expected. Cruickshank suggests that this delay was due to mixed acceptance and resistance to the concept of special education. Resistance came chiefly in the philosophy of progressive education. Progressive educators often advocated unplanned and heterogeneous grouping of children. This led to the demise of special classes and subsequent reassignment of handicapped children to regular classes, where they were mistreated or ignored. The end of World War II saw the demise of progressive education, together with an increase in the status of the teaching profession. During 1949 only 77 colleges gave sequences of courses in teaching exceptional children, but by 1953 this number had risen to 122.

The 1950s were the years of parent organizations, public awareness, demonstration programs, and legislative action. The founding convention of the National Association for Retarded Children (NARC) in 1950 marked the beginning of a new era. The development of NARC stimulated the growth and development of other local and state organizations. It also helped parents to find each other and led to a broad-based public education program that brought the subject of retardation out in the open.

One of the important activities of the 1950s was the plethora of new service programs established by associations like NARC. These programs provided two badly needed services: (1) they tried to meet the needs of retarded children and adults, and (2) they established demonstration models for public and voluntary community service agencies. According to the National Association for Retarded Citizens, needs of the retarded include:

1. Research leading to prevention and better treatment
2. Early identification
3. Parent and family education
4. Improved educational opportunity
5. Increased number of trained personnel to work with retarded citizens
6. Career development and vocational options for retarded citizens
7. Continued emphasis on societal integration, not exclusion, for retarded citizens
8. Extending and improving opportunities for sheltered employment of those incapable of entering the competitive employment market
9. Modifying laws governing the civil status of retarded citizens
10. Where needed, development of residential facilities close to the mainstream of community life
11. Effective planning and coordination of public and private activities at national, regional, state, and local levels.

During the mid 1950s, major developments at the national legislative level occurred under the auspices of Senator Lister Hill of Alabama and Congressman John Fogarty of Rhode Island. They introduced and steered to enactment legislation, both substantive and budgetary, that aided the handicapped.

The 1960s were the years of executive leadership under President Kennedy at the national level, comprehensive mental retardation planning at the state level, and discovery of new service concepts in Europe. In 1961, President Kennedy appointed a panel on mental retardation. A report, issued a year later by this committee, suggested that mental retardation was a matter of national concern. They further suggested that the federal government had an obligation to provide and stimulate services for retarded citizens. One outgrowth of the panel's work was the preparation by states of comprehensive plans for meeting the needs of the retarded.

In 1961, the Board of Education of the state of Washington gave new scope to the established jargon. During that year, the state legislature attempted to put restraints on the expenditure of funds for education in state residential facilities for the mentally retarded. By specifying that funds appropriated to the state superintendent of public instructions might be spent for handicapped pupils in the state institutions only for "children who meet the criteria of educability to be established by the state board of education," the state board responded to the challenge by formulating the following definition of educability: "A child shall be deemed educable if he possesses the potential to respond to and benefit from educational experiences in terms of such factors as social competence, emotional stability, self care, vocational competency or intellectual growth." This definition was interpreted by parents and superintendents of facilities for the retarded as one which included all children.

Finally, a "declaration of the general and special rights of the mentally retarded" was adopted by the International League of Societies for the Mentally Handicapped in 1968. This document gave international recognition to the concept of "rights" and set a standard for positive thinking about retarded citizens. Some statements relative to special education include the following:

Article I: The mentally retarded person has the same basic rights as other citizens of the same age and country.

Article II: The mentally retarded person has a right to proper medical care and physical restoration and to such education, training, habilitation and guidance as will enable him to develop his ability and potential to the fullest possible extent no matter how severe his degree of disability. No mentally handicapped person should be deprived of such services by reason of the cost involved.

The United Nations General Assembly adopted a resolution on December 20, 1971, declaring the rights of mentally retarded persons. Similarly, the Council for Exceptional Children at its 1971 convention adopted a policy statement which maintained that education is the right of all children. During the seventies, the courts, several states, and ultimately federal law mandated a free, appropriate public education for all handicapped children.

REVOLUTION

Federal Legislation and the Handicapped

"Federal legislation has been the single most significant incident in the total history of special education" (Reynolds and Rosen, 1976).

The purpose of this section is to review the major pieces of federal legislation that have had an impact on special education for the handicapped. The first attempt by the federal government to deal with special education occurred in 1864 when President Lincoln signed a law providing federal money to start Gallaudet College (Weintraub, 1971). Prior to this time, the federal government apparently played no active role in supporting special education.

In 1879, Congress authorized ten thousand dollars to the American Printing House for the Blind to produce braille materials. Gallaudet and the American Printing House represented the sum of federal involvement until 1918. During that year, the Soldiers' Rehabilitation Act was passed. The law provided for the physical and vocational rehabilitation of veterans. The scars of war prodded the government to improve services for handicapped veterans. The intent of this law was later broadened to include other handicapped citizens. Specifically, in 1920, the Smith-Fess Act extended services provided to handicapped veterans to civilian handicapped.

The period of 1921 to 1958 was a quiet one for the federal government in special education. While some legislation was passed, it was primarily for the blind. However, in 1931, a Section on Exceptional Children and Youth was established in the United States Office of Education (USOE). According to Weintraub, this section had no specific legislative or fiscal authority, but it laid the foundation for future federal involvement in special education.

In 1954, President Eisenhower signed the Cooperative Research Act (P.L. 83-531), which authorized cooperative research in education. In passing this law, Congress acknowledged the need for federal aid to support and encourage appropriate education for handicapped children.

In 1961, P.L. 87-276 was passed establishing training grants for teachers, rather than leadership personnel, in education of the deaf. This increased the number of teachers trained under university auspices. However, the number of qualified doctoral-level personnel with training in this area was no more than a dozen (Connor, 1976).

The deaf and blind were serviced first, both by special education and the federal government. Congress was interested in working with the deaf and passed legislation authorizing programs for the deaf to be administered by the USOE. This legislation included establishment of a nationwide loan service of captioned films for the deaf and provision of fellowships through grants to colleges and universities to train personnel to teach the deaf (Weintraub, 1971).

In 1963, President Kennedy signed P.L. 88-164 into law. This law provided for the organization of the Division of Handicapped Children and Youth in the USOE. This law centralized administration of the captioned films program, an expanded teacher-training program, and a program devoted to research. Research and development centers were established in several large universities. Research in these centers included a focus on early childhood education, learning characteristics of handicapped children, curriculum and materials development, and innovations in teacher education.

In 1965, P.L. 89-313 was enacted. This law was titled Federal Assistance to State Operated and Supported Schools for the Handicapped. This law amended Title I of the Elementary and Secondary Act of 1964, which firmly established the role of the federal government in aid to education. This law established grants to state agencies for providing free public education to handicapped children. Title I of this law provided services for disadvantaged handicapped children. Title II gave financial support to supplemental centers and also encouraged development of innovative programs for handicapped children.

During the period of the early sixties, dramatic changes took place in public education for the handicapped. The shift was from exclusion of the handicapped in public education to inclusion and integration. Compulsory education laws often served as a vehicle for excluding handicapped children from school. For example, Alaska law condoned exclusion of children with bodily or mental conditions rendering attendance inadvisable. Nevada law provided for exclusion of the children where physical or mental condition or attitude was such as to present or render inadvisable their attendance at school or application to study (Weintraub and Abeson, 1971).

Several factors contributed to the dramatic changes in attitude that occurred in the sixties. They include:

1. Parent group pressure on education
2. Professional organization activity
3. Court cases
4. President Kennedy's leadership
5. Social consciousness and upheaval
6. Political and legal activity on behalf of the handicapped

In 1965, Congress passed the Elementary and Secondary Education Act (P.L. 89-10). Title I of this act provided money to school systems to aid disadvantaged children: "In recognition of the special education needs of children of low income families and the impact that concentrations of low income families have on the ability of local education agencies to support educational programs, the title provides financial assistance to local education agencies for the education of children of low income families" (Section 101). Public Law 89-313, passed November of 1965, amended Title I to provide grants to state agencies directly responsible for providing free public education for handicapped children. The benefits of this law were also applicable to children from state institutions for the handicapped. Title III of P.L. 89-10 also had an impact on the handicapped. It provided funds for the establishment or expansion of exemplary and innovative programs including special programs for handicapped children.

The United States House of Representatives formed a subcommittee in 1966 to assess the educational needs of handicapped children and the extent to which the federal government was involved in meeting these needs. The findings of this committee were included in the 1966 amendments to the ESEA, P.L. 89-750. Grants-in-aid to states for special education were established by these amendments.

The Bureau of Education for the Handicapped (BEH) was established within the USOE in 1967. The research branch of BEH was funded at a level over eight million dollars in 1967, with large increases planned for the future. During 1967, more than twenty-four million dollars were allocated to colleges, universities, and state departments of education. This money was used to support pre-service and in-service training of researchers and administrators of special education.

In September of 1968, Congress passed the Handicapped Children's Early Education Assistance Act, P.L. 90-538. This act demonstrated that Congress was willing to pass specific legislation for the benefit of handicapped children. This law provided funds for the establishment of experimental demonstration centers for the education of preschool handicapped children. The Ninetieth Congress also amended three other general education laws to help handicapped children. First, Congress mandated that 15 percent of Title III ESEA monies must be spent for special education. Second, Congress mandated that 10 percent of state grant funds under the Vocational Education Act of 1963 be used for special education purposes. Third, Congress amended the Higher Education Facilities Act of 1963 because of concern that qualified handicapped students were being denied program accessability in higher education.

The period from 1969 to 1972 was relatively quiet in terms of federal involvement with special education. However, some laws bearing on the handicapped were passed. In 1969, Congress passed P.L. 91-61. The purpose of this law was to provide for a National Center on Educational Media and Materials for the Handicapped and for other purposes. In June of 1972, Congress passed P.L. 92-318, known as the Education Amendments of 1972. In 1973, Congress passsed P.L. 93-42. This law provided for the establishment of a National Autistic Children's Week.

In 1973, Congress passed P.L. 93-112, the Rehabilitation Act of 1973, which has been called a civil rights act for the handicapped. In general, the last section of P.L. 93-112, Section 504, is most important for handicapped citizens. This law says that no recipient of federal funds can discriminate against an otherwise handicapped person solely based on his handicap. The mandate applies to preschool, elementary, and secondary public education programs, as well as any other programs or activities that receive any federal financial assistance, according to the regulations promulgated by that agency to implement Section 504.

In 1974, Congress passed P.L. 93-380. This law was called the Education of the Handicapped Amendments of 1974 and was an amendment to Title III of the Elementary and Secondary Education Act of 1965 (P.L. 89-10). This law directed the Commissioner of

Education to "carry out a program for making grants for supplementary education centers and assist in the provision of vitally needed educational services not available in sufficient quantity or quality, and to stimulate and assist in the development and establishment of exemplary elementary and secondary school educational programs to serve as models for regular school programs" (Section 301).

In 1975, Congress passed P.L. 94-142. This law is also known as the Education for All Handicapped Children Act. This law required each participating state to establish a policy that assures all handicapped children a free, appropriate public education. Furthermore, the state must develop a plan for achieving this goal. The law also required states to maximize equal educational opportunity for all handicapped children between the ages of 3 and 21 by September 1, 1980.

Court Cases

The enactment of P.L. 94-142 represents a milestone in the history of education for handicapped children. Many factors contributed to the development of this legislation, but none was more important than the landmark court cases.

The importance of education was clearly established in the *Brown* case. The Supreme Court found that racial segregation in public education was a violation of the Fourteenth Amendment. The fact that this case is cited in nearly every related decision since 1954 attests to its profound impact. The court said:

> Education is required in the performance of our basic responsibilities
> . . . . It is the very foundation of good citizenship. It is a principal instrument for awakening the child to cultural values, in preparing him for later . . . training, and in helping him to adjust normally to his environment. It is doubtful that any child may reasonably be expected to succeed in life if he is denied the opportunity of an education. Today, education is perhaps the most important function of the state and local governments . . . . Where the state has undertaken to provide it, it is a right which must be available to all on equal terms.

The defendants in the *Brown* case agreed that black children were educated in separate classes. However, they claimed that these separate educational facilities were equal to those that white children attended.

The court was not convinced. They said essentially that while education is a state not a federal responsibility, it is a service that must be provided to all citizens on an equal basis. Furthermore, separate is inherently unequal and discriminatory.

Turnbull (1978) suggests that attorneys for handicapped children have maintained, citing *Brown*, that their clients have the same right to education as non-handicapped students. He says their complaint has two elements: (1) there is differential treatment among and within the class of handicapped children, and (2) some handicapped children are denied an education while non-handicapped children receive it. Finally, these representatives suggest that all children, including the handicapped, have a constitutional right to a public education.

The *Brown* decision established the finding that all the members of a particular class of people are covered by the Fourteenth Amendment. In *Brown*, the class includes racial minorities, while in the right-to-education cases the class includes handicapped students.

The period between 1954 and 1970 was for the most part a latent one in the area of landmark cases that would impact on the education of handicapped children. However, it was a time of active parent organization, federal intervention, evolution of more and better professional preparation programs, research, etc. However, this was truly a period of calm before the storm. The storm began with the *Pennsylvania Association for Retarded Children (PARC)* case. This case signalled the beginning of the end for educational discrimination against handicapped children.

Seventeen years after Brown, in 1971, this issue was raised again, but this time the class was not black children, it was handicapped children. The questions were similar:

1. Do handicapped children have a right to a free public education?
2. Is separate education for handicapped children inherently unequal?
3. What is "education" for a handicapped student?
4. Do handicapped children have due process rights?

In January, 1971, PARC brought suit against the Commonwealth of Pennsylvania for the state's failure to provide all retarded children with a free public education. The plaintiffs included fourteen mentally retarded children of school age who represented themselves and all other school-age retarded children in Pennsylvania. The defendants in the case included the state secretaries of education and public welfare, the state board of education, and thirteen school districts, which represented all of Pennsylvania's school districts.

The suit specifically questioned public policy and practice that excluded, postponed, or denied free access to public education for retarded children who could benefit from such education. The fact that they could benefit was attested to by expert witnesses. These experts developed three specific conclusions. First, the provision of systematic education programs to mentally retarded children will produce learning. Second, education cannot be defined solely as the provision of academic experiences to children, it must be seen as a continuous process by which individuals learn to cope and function with their environment. For retarded children to learn to feed and clothe themselves is a legitimate outcome of an educational program. Third, the earlier these children are provided with educational experiences, the greater the amount of learning that can be predicted. It should also be mentioned here that Pennsylvania had statutory language that made education available to all children in the commonwealth. The clear denial of education to the plaintiffs in PARC was therefore a violation of state statute.

The suit was resolved by a stipulation and order in June, 1971 and in October by a consent agreement and order. The June stipulation stated that retarded children cannot be denied access to a free public education without due process of law. The October decree provided that Pennsylvania could not apply any law that would postpone, terminate, or deny mentally retarded children access to a publicly supported education. The court said that by October, 1971, the plaintiffs were to have been re-evaluated and placed in programs, and, by September, 1972, all retarded children between the ages of six and twenty-one must be provided a publicly supported education. The court further mandated that local districts that provide pre-school education to any children must provide the same service for retarded children. The decree also said that it was desirable to educate retarded children in a program most like that provided for non-handicapped children.

In summary, the PARC case provided the following guidelines

for educating retarded children:

1. All retarded children are entitled to a free public education.
2. The definition of education is not limited to academic experiences but is seen as a continuous process by which individuals learn to cope and function in their environment.
3. Placement in a regular class is preferable to any special class for these children.
4. Parents are entitled to a hearing before any change in the educational program for their retarded child is made.
5. Postponement or termination of educational programming is prohibited unless a hearing takes place.
6. Retarded children must be re-evaluated on a regular basis.

In PARC, the court found that education is critical if one is to successfully function in society and that retarded children can benefit from education. Furthermore, this right to an education is protected by the Fifth and Fourteenth Amendments of the Constitution.

In 1972, the court in the *Mills* case reiterated the above statements and expanded the coverage to all handicapped children in the District of Columbia. In *Mills*, the parents and guardians of seven District of Columbia children brought a class action suit against the Board of Education of the District, the Department of Human Resources, and the mayor for failure to provide all children with a publicly supported education.

The children ranged in age from seven to sixteen and were alleged by the school to have certain problems: slightly brain damaged, hyperactive, epileptic, mentally retarded, and orthopedically handicapped. Because of these problems, the children received no public education. Another issue in this case was the manner in which these children were denied entrance to or were excluded from public education programs. The complaint said that "Plaintiffs were so excluded without a formal determination of the basis for their exclusion and without provision for periodic review of their status." It was also pointed out that:

> . . . the procedures by which plaintiffs were excluded or suspended from public school are arbitrary and do not conform to the due process requirements of the Fifth Amendment. Plaintiffs are excluded and suspended without: (a) notification as to a hearing, the nature of offense or status, any alternative or interim publicly supported education; (b) op-

portunity for representation, a hearing by an impartial arbiter, the presentation of witnesses; and (c) opportunity for periodic review of the necessity for continued exclusion or suspension.

On December 20, 1971, the court issued a stipulated agreement and order. The defendants failed to comply with this order, resulting in plaintiffs filing a motion in January, 1972 for summary judgment and a proposed order and decree for implementation of the proposed judgment. In August, 1972, United States District Judge Joseph Waddy issued such an order and decree providing:

1. A declaration of the consitutional rights of all children . . . to a publicly supported education.
2. A declaration that the defendants . . . policies which excluded children denied . . . plaintiffs . . . rights of due process and equal protection of the law.

The defendants claimed that it would be impossible for them to afford plaintiffs the relief sought unless the Congress appropriated needed funds. The court responded:

> The defendants are required by the Constitution of the United States, the District of Columbia Code, and their own regulations to provide a publicly supported education for these 'exceptional' children. Their failure to fulfill this clear duty to include and retain these children in the public school system, or otherwise provide them with publicly supported education, and their failure to afford them due process hearings and periodic review, cannot be excused by the claim that there are insufficient funds. . . . If sufficient funds are not available to finance all of the services and programs that are needed and desirable in the system, then the available funds must be expended equitably in such a manner that no child is entirely excluded from a publicly supported education consistent with his needs and ability to benefit therefrom. . . .

According to Martin (1977), the successful resolution of the *PARC* and *Mills* cases led to thirty-six right-to-education decisions in twenty-seven states. The influence and impact of these decisions on federal legislation (P.L. 94-142, Sec. 504) was critical. They helped to point the way into the future.

Studying the decision in the *Mills* case leads one to another landmark case, *Hobson* v. *Hansen*. This was a class action brought on behalf of black school children in Washington D.C. The defendants were the school superintendent as well as other school officials. The legal basis for the claim alleged that the tracking system of educational placement operated invidiously against blacks and poor students, depriving them of an equal educational opportunity. This then violated the Fourteenth Amendment of the Constitution. The court rendered a decision in 1967: "Judge Wright found that denying poor public school children educational opportunities equal to that available to more affluent public school children was violating the Due Process Clause of the Fifth Amendment. *A fortiori*, defendants' conduct here, denying plaintiffs and their class not just an equal publicly supported education but all publicly supported education while providing such education to other children is violative of the Due Process Clause."

As early then as 1967, the court in *Hobson* v. *Hansen* was suggesting that education is important and it must be made available to all children regardless of their social class. The court in *Mills* cites both *Hobson* v. *Hansen* and *Brown*.

Another landmark case dealt with evaluation and subsequent placement of children in special education classes. *Diana* was a class action suit brought on behalf of Mexican-American children in educable mentally retarded classes in California in 1970. The plaintiffs claimed that standardized intelligence tests, specifically the Stanford-Binet and the Wechsler, were written entirely in English. However, these tests were given to children whose primary language was not English. This constitutes a violation of the Equal Protection Clause of the Fourteenth Amendment.

This case was settled out of court with the following stipulations:

1. All children whose primary home language is other than English. . . must be tested in both the primary language and English.
2. Mexican-American and Chinese children in classes for the mentally retarded must be re-tested in their primary language.
3. Any school district which had a sufficient disparity between the percentage of Mexican-American students in their regular classes and its classes for the retarded had to submit an explanation citing the reasons for this disparity.

The basic issue regarding testing and placement of children in special education classes raised by this case was dealt with by P.L. 94-142. The law requires that children must be tested in their primary language and stipulates that no single test may be the sole criterion for determining a child's educational program or placement.

The basic issue raised in the *Diana* case was expanded in the case of *Larry P.* v. *Riles* (1972). The plaintiffs here alleged that they were inappropriately classified as educable mentally retarded on the basis of tests which failed to recognize their unfamiliarity with white middle-class culture. They further claimed that the testing ignored the value of black culture.

On October 10, 1979, Judge Peckham handed down his final decision in the case of *Larry P.* v. *Riles*. The court found that the use of IQ tests violated Title VI of the Civil Rights Act of 1964, the Rehabilitation Act of 1973, and the Education for All Handicapped Children Act of 1975. The court also stated that the use of IQ tests violates state and federal constitutional guarantees of the equal protection of the laws.

Based on these findings, the court made permanent the original temporary injunction prohibiting the use of any standardized intelligence tests for the identification of black educable mentally retarded children or their placement into educable mentally retarded classes.

Future

With the enactment of P.L. 94-142 and Section 504, public policy toward the handicapped has undergone a dramatic shift. Society's obligation and commitment to provide a free, appropriate public education for all handicapped children has become national policy. The base for this policy rests with the principles of equal opportunity and equal protection and is reflected in both federal and state laws. We have come a long way but where do we go from here?

Two options for the future seem possible: (1) continued forward progress until the full potential of every handicapped citizen is realized and (2) regression, retrenchment and stagnancy.

We are living in a period dominated by conservative thinking. The cries of belt-tightening, back to basics, and competency testing are frequently heard.

The role of education will be a critical factor in determining what the future will bring. During the last ten years, policy change in special education was dominated by the courts and governmental policymakers (Higgins and Barresi, 1979). The courts and government have told educators what to do. This seems to be a sad commentary on education, which has taken a back seat in this process.

Educators must take a more active leadership role in the future. If they do not, the courts and government policymakers, not educators, will lead us in the eighties as they did in the seventies.

REFERENCES

Aiello, B.: Especially for special educators: A sense of our own history. *Exceptional Children, 42*(5):244-252, 1976.

Connor, F.P.: The past is prologue: Teacher preparation in special education. *Exceptional Children, 42*(7):366-381, 1976.

Heiny, R.: Special education: History. In Deighton, L.C. (Ed.): *Encyclopedia of Education.* New York: Macmillan, 1971, vol. 8.

Higgins, S., and Barresi, J.: The changing focus of public policy. *Exceptional Children, 45*(4):270-284, 1979.

LaVor, M.: Federal legislation for exceptional persons: A history. In Weintraub, Frederick J. et al. (Eds.): *Public Policy and the Education of Exceptional Children.* Reston, Virginia: Council for Exceptional Children, 1976.

Lippman, I., and Goldberg, I.I.: *Right to Education.* New York: Teachers College Press, 1973.

Martin, R.: *Educational Rights of Handicapped Children.* Champaign, Illinois: Research Press Company, 1977.

Preen, Brian: *Schooling for the Mentally Retarded: An Historical Perspective.* New York: St. Martin's Press, 1977.

Reynolds, M., and Rosen: Special education: Past, present and future. *Educational Forum, 15*(4):551-562, 1976.

Shaw, C.R., and Lucas, A.R.: *The Psychiatric Disorders of Childhood.* New York: Appleton-Century-Crofts, 1970.

Turnbull, H.R., and Turnbull, A.: *Free Appropriate Public Education.* Denver: Love Publishing Company, 1978.

Weintraub, F.J.: Special education and the government. In Deighton, L.C. (Ed.): *Encyclopedia of Education.* New York: Macmillan, 1971, vol. 8.

Weintraub, F.J., and Abeson, A.R.: Appropriate education for all handicapped children: A growing issue. 1037-1058, *Syracuse Law Review, 23*(4), 1972.

Federal Laws

The Education for All Handicapped Children Act, Public Law No. 94-142, 20, U.S.C. 1401, et seq.

The Rehabilitation Act of 1973, Public Law No. 93-112, 29 U.S.C. 794.

Education Amendments of 1974, Public Law No. 93-380.

National Autistic Children's Week, Public Law No. 93-42.

Education Amendments of 1972, Public Law No. 92-318.

To Provide for a National Center on Educational Media and Materials for the Handicapped, Public Law No. 91-61.

Handicapped Children's Early Education Assistance Act, Public Law No. 90-538.

Elementary and Secondary Education Act Amendments of 1966, Public Law No. 89-750.

Elementary and Secondary Education Act of 1965, as amended, Public Law No. 89-10.

Federal Assistance to State Operated and Supported Schools for the Handicapped, Public Law No. 89-313.

Mental Retardation Facilities and Community Mental Health Centers Construction Act of 1963, Public Law No. 88-164.

To make available...specially trained teachers of the deaf..., Public Law No. 87-276.

To authorize cooperative research in education, Public Law No. 83-531.

Cases

Brown v. Board of Education, 347 U.S. 483 (1954).

Diana et al. v. State Board of Education, United States District Court, Northern District of California, C-70 37 RFP, 1969.

Hobson v. Hansen, 269, F. Supp. 401 (1967).

Larry, P. et al. v. Wilson Riles et al., United States District Court, Northern District of California, No. C-71 2270 RFP, Order and Memorandum.

Mills v. Board of Education of the District of Columbia, 348 F. Supp 866 (D.C.C. 1972).

Pennsylvania Association for Retarded Children v. Pennsylvania, 343 F. Supp. 279 (E.D. Pa., 1972).

Chapter 2

LAWS AND SPECIAL EDUCATION: P.L. 94-142, SECTION 504 AND MASSACHUSETTS CHAPTER 766

Introduction

TODAY, special education is under attack at both the federal and state level. This attack seems to be especially severe at the federal level under Reaganomics and the "New Federalism."

One strategy that concerned professionals and citizens can utilize in order to protect the gains that have been made for the handicapped over the last ten years is to clearly understand the following laws: (1) P.L. 94-142, The Education for All Handicapped Children Act of 1975, (2) P.L. 93-112, Section 504, The Rehabilitation Act of 1973, and (3) Chapter 766, The Massachusetts State Special Education Law of 1972.

The first two are federal laws that apply throughout the United States; Chapter 766 applies only in Massachusetts, but it served as a prototype for P.L. 94-142.

In general these three laws can be identified in the following manner:

1. P.L. 94-142 is basically a funding law
2. Section 504 is basically a civil rights law
3. Chapter 766 is basically a state special education law

P.L. 94-142, Education of the Handicapped Act

The Education for All Handicapped Children Act, P.L. 94-142, was the landmark education statute passed by Congress during the decade of the seventies. The law, phased in over a four-year period (1978-1982), requires a free appropriate public education for all handicapped children ages three to twenty-one. In order to implement the "free, appropriate public education" mandate, a number of procedural requirements were enumerated.

Each handicapped child must have a multidisciplinary team evaluation, the results of which are used to develop an individualized education program (IEP). The IEP is a written document that must be revised annually at a meeting in which the child's parents must participate.

The IEP must specify the child's present level of performance, annual and short-term goals for instruction, services to be provided, a schedule of implementation, and criteria for evaluating pupil progress.

Services to the handicapped child must be provided in the "least restrictive environment" so that handicapped children are educated with normal children to the maximum extent educationally appropriate.

Parents and children have a variety of due process rights to challenge school systems regarding assessment, identification, placement, and educational program recommendations for handicapped children.

Required compliance with P.L. 94-142 differs from many federal programs in which the worst sanction would be termination of funds for that program. Because the rules for P.L. 94-142 have been coordinated and interrelated with P.L. 93-112 (a civil rights act), noncompliance could result in termination of all federal funds.

P.L. 93-112, Rehabilitation Acts of 1973, Section 504

The Rehabilitation Acts of 1973, P.L. 93-112, has been referred to as a civil rights act for the handicapped. Section 504 of the law says: "No otherwise qualified handicapped individual in the United States, shall, solely by reason of his handicap, be excluded from the participation in, be denied the benefits of, or be subjected to discrimination under any program or activity receiving federal financial assistance."

Subpart D of Section 504 deals with non-discrimination in elementary and secondary education. The requirements contained here are virtually identical to P.L. 94-142 requirements.

It is important to remember that Section 504 requirements are broader than those contained in P.L. 94-142, which deals only with education. Moreover, non-compliance with Section 504 violates a civil rights act and therefore could jeopardize all federal funds to a state or local community.

Chapter 766, Massachusetts State Special Education Law

In 1972, the Massachusetts legislature passed a law (Ch. 766) that was and continues to be the most comprehensive state special education law in the country. Regulations for the law were promulgated in 1974. In many ways, Chapter 766 is the same as P.L. 94-142. Major components of both laws include the following:

1. Highest priority is given to individuals not currently receiving service or those inadequately served.
2. Guaranteed safeguards of due process rights of parents and children, including the right to protest decisions of school officials.
3. Least restrictive environment. That is, handicapped students must be educated to the maximum extent educationally appropriate with non-handicapped students.
4. Student evaluation must be racially and culturally non-discriminatory.
5. Individualized educational plans must be developed for each handicapped child and parents must be part of the team that devises the plan.
6. If students are placed in private schools, the local school district must pay.

In some areas, Chapter 766 was stricter than P.L. 94-142. For example, evaluation of student progress was required four times per year (recently this was changed to twice a year), but P.L. 94-142 only requires evaluation once a year.

The next section of this chapter will be a detailed point-by-point comparison of the three laws.

Recent developments at the federal and state level may have a significant impact on the future of P.L. 94-142, P.L. 93-112 Section 504, and Chapter 766.

P.L. 94-142. The effectiveness and appropriateness of P.L. 94-142 has been challenged by the following documents:

1. A United States General Accounting Office (GAO) report issued on 2/5/81, entitled "Unanswered Questions on Educating Handicapped Children in Local Public Schools."
2. A GAO report issued on 9/30/81, entitled "Disparities Still Exist in Who Gets Special Education."
3. A report issued by OSE, entitled "Briefing Paper: Initial Review of Regulations Under Part B of the Education of the Handicapped Act, As Amended."
   (This document is a working paper with respect to issuance of new P.L. 94-142 regulations.)

SECTION 504. One of President Reagan's basic campaign promises was to get the government off the back of the people. This was to be achieved by eliminating unnecessary and burdensome federal regulations. In fact, one of Vice President Bush's major responsibilities has been to oversee the effort to deregulate. Finally, one of the first and foremost targets for deregulation is Section 504.

MASSACHUSETTS CHAPTER 766. Recently, Massachusetts issued a report entitled "Implementing Massachusetts Special Education Law: A Statewide Assessment." This report provides some thoughtful and interesting insights into the implementation and effectiveness of Chapter 766.

P.L. 94-142

I. "UNANSWERED QUESTIONS ON EDUCATING HANDICAPPED CHILDREN IN LOCAL PUBLIC SCHOOLS." This report, issued on 2/5/81, is critical of P.L. 94-142 and focuses its criticism on five specific areas: (1) the number of children needing service, (2) eligibility criteria, (3) individualized education programs, (4) sufficiency of resources, and (5) program management and enforcement. The report claims that a large difference exists between the Department of Education's (DOE) 1974 estimate of number of handicapped children

LAW	P.L. 94 – 142	MASS. CH. 766	P.L. 93 – 112 SEC. 504
	FUNDING	SPECIAL EDUCATION	CIVIL RIGHTS
General Purpose of the Law	Established the right of every American child, including the most severely handicapped, to a free, appropriate public education in the least restrictive environment.	Established the right of every Massachusetts child, including the most severely handicapped, to a free, appropriate public education in the least restrictive environment.	Discrimination on the basis of handicap is prohibited in: 1. Pre-school, elementary and secondary education 2. Post-secondary education 3. Program accessibility 4. Employment practices 5. Health, welfare, and social services.
Dates — Statute	November 29, 1975	1972	September 26, 1973
Regulations	August 23, 1977	May 28, 1974	May 4, 1977
Jurisdiction	USA	Massachusetts only	USA
Monitoring	U.S. Dept. of Education — Office of Sp. Ed. and Rehab. Services	State Education Agency — Intermediate Education Agency — Local Education Agency	U.S. Dept. of Education — Office of Civil Rights

LAW	P.L. 94 – 142	MASS. CH. 766	P.L. 93 – 112 SEC. 504
Compliance	Optional *New Mexico does not participate *Same requirements in 504	Mandatory and Monitored	Mandatory and Monitored by Office for Civil Rights
Penalty for Non-compliance	No funding through Part B	Withholding of State re-imbursement under Ch. 70	Potential withholding of all Federal funds to SEA, LEA, etc.
Funds for Special Education	Yes	Yes	No
Testing Requirements	1. Tests must be selected and administered in a non-discriminatory manner. 2. Students must be tested in their native language or mode of communication. 3. No single test may be the sole criteria for determining a child's program or placement.	Same as 94 – 142	Same as 94 – 142
Age of Students Serviced	3 – 21 years	3 – 21 years	3 – 21 years
Individualized Educational Plan Required	Yes	Yes	Yes

LAW	P.L. 94–142	MASS. CH. 766	P.L. 93–112 SEC. 504
Review of Student Progress	Once a year	Twice a year	Same as P.L. 94–142
Procedural Safeguards	Yes	Yes	Yes
Free, Appropriate Public Education	Required	Required	Required
Eligibility	Any handicapped child age 3–21	Any handicapped child age 3–21	No otherwise qualified handicapped person age 3–21 may be discriminated against in school programs.
Definition of Handicapped Student	*1. Deaf 2. Deaf-Blind 3. Hard of hearing 4. Mentally retarded 5. Multihandicapped 6. Orthopedically impaired 7. Other health impaired 8. Seriously emotionally disturbed 9. Specific learning disability 10. Speech impaired 11. Visually handicapped *Each of the above categories is defined in Sec. 12/a.5 of the regulations.	A child who, because of temporary or more permanent adjustment difficulties or attributes arising from intellectual, sensory, emotional or physical factors, cerebral dysfunctions, perceptual factors, or other specific learning impairments, or any combination thereof, is unable to progress effectively in a regular education program and requires special education. (Sec. 103.0 of the regulations)	Broad definition which includes any person who has a physical or mental impairment which substantially limits one or more major life activities, such as the functions of caring for one's self, performing manual tasks, walking, seeing, hearing, speaking, breathing, learning, and working.

LAW	P.L. 94 – 142	MASS. CH. 766	P.L. 93 – 112 SEC. 504
Definition of Special Education	Specially designed instruction, at no cost to the parent, to meet the unique needs of a handicapped child, including classroom instruction, instruction in physical education, home instruction and instruction in hospitals and institutions. (Sec. 121a.14)	Everything which is required to be provided to a child in need of special education pursuant to the IEP for such a child. (Sec. 122.0)	Special education includes related aids and services that are designed to meet the individual educational needs of handicapped persons as adequately as the needs of non-handicapped persons are met. (Sec. 84.33 /b/)
IEP	1. Statement of child's present level of educational performance. 2. Statement of annual goals, including short-term instructional objectives. 3. Statement of specific special education and related services to be provided to the child and the extent to which child will participate in regular educational programs. 4. Projected dates for initiation of services and anticipated duration of services. 5. Appropriate objective criteria and evaluation procedures and schedules for determining, on at least an annual basis,	1. Statement of what child can do. 2. Statement of measurable physical constraints on performance. 3. Statement of child's learning style. 4. Statement of general educational objectives. 5. Statement of suggested methodology and teaching approach for meeting general objectives. 6. Statement of types and amounts of services. 7. Statement of any parent-child instruction. 8. Statement of physical education services for the child.	Sec. 504 requires each recipient of federal funds to provide an education which includes services designated to meet handicapped persons individual needs as adequately as non-handicapped persons. According to the regulations, an IEP will meet the requirement.

LAW	P.L. 94 – 142	MASS. CH. 766	P.L. 93 – 112 SEC. 504
IEP (continued)	whether the short-term instructional objectives are being achieved. (Sec. 121a. 346)	9. Statement of any specialized equipment and materials. 10. Statement regarding daily duration of child's program. 11. Statement regarding the number of days per year on which program will be provided. 12. Statement regarding child's transportation needs. 13. Criteria for child's movement to next less restrictive prototype. (Sec. 322.1)	
Placement in the Least Restrictive Environment	Sec. 121a. 550 – 556 of P.L. 94 – 142 regulations requires SEA to insure: 1. That handicapped students are educated with non-handicapped students in public schools to the maximum extent possible and appropriate to their needs. 2. Removal of handicapped students from the regular education environment occurs only when the nature of the handicap is such that education in the regular class cannot be achieved satisfactorily.	"Least Restrictive Prototype" The program that to the maximum extent appropriate allows a child to be educated with children who are not in need of special education. (Sec. 111.0 of the regulations)	Sec. 84.34 of the 504 regulations requires the SEA to provide for the education of each qualified handicapped person and to place each handicapped person in a regular educational environment unless it can demonstrate that this cannot be achieved satisfactorily even with.

LAW	P.L. 94-142	MASS. CH. 766	P.L. 93-112 SEC. 504
Continuum of Services	Deno Cascade Model	Program Prototypes 502.1 Reg. class with mod. .2 25% out .3 60% out .4 Sub. separate .5 Day school .6 Residential .7 Home, hospital of regional adolescent program .8 Programs for ages 3–4 .9 Diagnostic program .10 General .11 Programs for ages 16–21	Deno Cascade Model

needing service (about 6.2 million) and the number of children actually receiving service (as of December, 1979, only 4 million). Two possible explanations for this discrepancy are suggested. The GAO says that the original DOE estimates of the number of handicapped children needing service were inaccurate. The DOE says that the children are there but states are not finding them. In spite of which of these theories is correct, the data have hurt the credibility of DOE statistics and also, by implication, P.L. 94-142 funding needs.

The report also claims that approximately one-third of the children counted as handicapped were classified as speech impaired and were receiving only speech therapy. The report goes on to charge that many of these speech-impaired children were stutterers, lispers, or guilty of unpleasant voice tone. DOE regulations require that children receiving only speech therapy must pass an "adverse effect" test to qualify for federal funds. In July, 1980, the DOE solved this problem by suggesting that any child meets the adverse effect test if he or she is receiving speech therapy.

Public Law 94-142 requires an individualized education plan for each handicapped child. However, the GAO report uncovered a number of problems with IEP, in that 84 percent of those reviewed lacked (1) one or more of the required items of information, (2) evidence that parents or other required participants attended planning meetings, and (3) were not prepared until after prescribed deadlines.

The report found that in spite of significant movement toward compliance, local education officials did not expect to comply with the laws mandated until 3 to 6 years beyond 1978. The most frequent explanation for this delay was inadequate funding.

Finally, the report cites a number of additional management problems inhibiting the implementation of the law. These include:

1. Insufficient staff at the state level to assist local education agencies and monitor their programs.
2. Delays by the DOE in issuing regulations, providing guidance and instructions, and approving state plans.
3. Lack of comprehensive federal evaluations of the states' compliance with the acts mandate.

II. "DISPARITIES STILL EXIST IN WHO GETS SPECIAL EDUCATION." This report was issued on September 30, 1981 and suggests that participation in special education depends on a set of interrelated factors, including the state in which the child lives, the child's handicapping condition, sex, minority status, and programs available in a school district. The report provides an in-depth analysis of the following questions:

1. What are the numbers and characteristics of children receiving special education?
2. Are there eligible children who are unserved or underserved?
3. Are certain types of children over-represented in special education programs?
4. What factors influence who gets special education?

In response to the first question, the following data are presented in the report:

- 8.5 percent of the school-age population is receiving special education. (The P.L. 94-142 funding formula assumes 12 percent exists.)
- Nearly 4.2 million children received special education during the 1980-81 school year.
- The typical child participating in special education is young, male, and mildly handicapped.
- Twice as many males as females receive special education.
- During the 1980-81 school year, 36 percent of those counted were learning disabled, 30 percent were speech impaired, and 19 percent mentally retarded.
- 13 percent of the children had severe handicaps, 36 percent had moderate handicaps, and 51 percent were mildly handicapped.

In response to the second question concerning the unserved or underserved, the following information was presented:

- The report suggests that states and local education agencies are finding few unserved children.
- Identified groups of underserved children include 3-5-year-olds, secondary school, and 18-21-year-olds, emotionally disturbed children, and migrant children. The report suggests that school dropouts may constitute an underserved population.

In response to the third question, the following data were presented:

- Learning disabled (LD) children exceed the number of children in any other category; in six states, LD children account for over half the handicapped children counted.

- A disproportionate share of minority children participate in some type of special education program.
- A disproportionate number of male children participate in some type of special education program.

In response to the fourth question, the following information was presented:

- Teacher attitudes and judgments play a large role in who gets referred to special education.
- State definitions of handicapping conditions and related eligibility criteria influence who gets special education.
- Some children are excluded from special education because of limits on school district programs relative to the need for services.

III. "BRIEFING PAPER: INITIAL REVIEW OF REGULATIONS UNDER PART B OF THE EDUCATION OF THE HANDICAPPED ACT AS AMENDED." This report was issued on September 1, 1981 and its stated purpose is to provide an overview of the deregulation process being implemented by the Office of Special Education and Rehabilitation Services and to present an initial discussion of targets of opportunity for deregulation currently identified in the Part B regulations.

Recommended areas for deregulation fall into four major categories:

1. Definitions. This includes the issue of defining LD as well as related services.
2. Grants administration. This includes state and local plans, allocation of funds, etc.
3. Services. Recommended changes here impact on many significant aspects of P.L. 94-142, including: free, appropriate public education, extended school year programs, suspension and expulsion, IEP, and CSPD.
4. Procedural safeguards. Recommended changes here would affect areas such as due process, non-discrimination in evaluation, least restrictive environment, and confidentiality of information.

The basic argument presented in this paper is this: a discrepancy exists between the statutory and regulatory provisions of P.L. 94-

142. In many instances, the regulatory requirements far exceed the intent of the statute. This results in an unnecessary burden on state and local education agencies, which should be alleviated.

The solution to this problem according to this document is to develop regulatory alternatives consistent with the statute, which will (1) relieve educational agencies of fiscal, paperwork, compliance and other burdens, (2) liberate public education agencies from unnecessary federal direction and control, and (3) decrease the number and impact of regulatory requirements.

This document will be a major factor influencing the issuance of new P.L. 94-142 regulations.

Section 504

While the historical importance of P.L. 94-142 cannot be overstated, it might be ignored and unenforceable without the backup of Section 504. Section 504 contains essentially the same educational requirements as does P.L. 94-142. The difference is in penalty for non-compliance and enforcement. The penalty for non-compliance with P.L. 94-142 is the loss of Part B monies. On the other hand, non-compliance with Section 504 may result in the withholding of "all" federal funds to a state or a local community. Enforcement of P.L. 94-142 is mainly handled by the Office of Special Education at the federal level and the state department of education at the state level. Section 504 (a civil rights act) is handled by the Federal Office of Civil Rights. Many people have looked on Section 504 as a "safety net" for P.L. 94-142. However, the current administration is attempting to weaken and de-regulate Section 504. The consequence of such action may be to severely weaken the P.L. 94-142 mandate.

A recurring theme echoed by President Reagan has been to get government off the back of the people. One way to do this, according to the president, is to eliminate unnecessary and burdensome federal regulations. To achieve this goal, the president asked Vice President Bush to head up a task force to study this problem.

One of the first laws to be scrutinized by Bush's committee was Section 504. As a result of work by this committee, the Justice Department has circulated a proposal to amend the Section 504 regulations.

An analysis of this proposal was reported in the February 10, 1982 edition of the newsletter *Education of the Handicapped*. A summary of the contents are as follows:

- Justice would drop most of the requirements in Section 504 that parallel those of P.L. 94-142.
- The draft would eliminate the part of the regulations that requires, whenever possible, handicapped children be educated alongside of children who are not handicapped.
- The revisions also would drop the requirements that schools have an appeals process for parents of handicapped children. . . .
- The reaction from advocates . . . was harsh. "Part of the administration's rhetoric in the past is that they can cut 94-142 because we have Section 504 to fall back on" said Stan Dublinske from ASHA.
- If these proposals are implemented, "it will be disastrous" said Reese Robrahn, executive director of the American Coalition of Citizens with Disabilities. "We don't think the philosophy of civil rights . . . has reached the point where every state will do it without federal regulations."
- The proposals would limit Section 504 coverage to programs that "receive" federal funds. The current regulations apply to programs that "receive" or "benefit from" federal funds. This is "perhaps the most devastating aspect of the entire proposal" said Reese Robrahn.

Massachusetts Chapter 766

Massachusetts has had in place a comprehensive special education law since 1974. However, the full impact of this statute has not previously been assessed. To this end, the Massachusetts State Department of Education commissioned a study to assess the impact of Chapter 766. Although this evaluation process is intended to be ongoing, a preliminary report was issued in April, 1982. The report is entitled "Implementing Massachusetts Special Education Law: A Statewide Assessment."

The report is detailed and lengthy, and only a summary will be reported here. The report focused on five study areas, which formed the basis of the evaluation strategy and the case studies. They were:

- the effects of Chapter 766 on regular education
- the effects of Chapter 766 on the provision of special education in the least restrictive appropriate setting
- the effects of Chapter 766 on the development of individual education plans
- the effects of Chapter 766 on secondary education
- the effects of fiscal funding issues on the implementation of Chapter 766

Summarizing the report according to the five study areas mentioned:

A. THE EFFECTS OF CHAPTER 766 ON REGULAR EDUCATION. The Gallup survey showed that 84 percent of the principals and 86 percent of regular education teachers believed that the quality of special education was better than ten years ago. At the onset of implementing Chapter 766, many teachers had expressed the concern that students would be placed in regular education classrooms. In actuality, students with profound handicaps were moved out of substandard facilities and a new set of programs were developed to meet their needs. They were not placed in regular education classrooms. Also, new programs were developed for students with learning and/or behavior problems. Students who spent part of their time both in these programs (usually resource rooms) and in the regular classroom and were carefully monitored by the special education staff in cooperation with the classroom teacher. The gap that had existed between regular and special education teachers was closed in many cases due to this cooperative effort.

The report did note, however, that despite overwhelming support for the concepts reflected in Chapter 766, special education became a scapegoat for the frustrations of many educators. There were often complaints concerning the paperwork and the cost. However, the report notes that the observers felt that these complaints might have been a cover-up for a deeper agenda, namely, job security in light of Proposition 2½, which limited the community's ability to raise taxes and therefore required reduction of staff. The report further suggested that special education had in a sense become a "lightning rod" for focusing the frustrations of educators. They offered three possible explanations, with one reinforcing the other: (1) public school education is generally under attack, (2) Chapter 766 is seen as an intrusion on local control, and (3) insecurity of regular education staff as a result of Proposition 2½.

Another area of concern is the inclination of educators to point to one or a few cases that have consumed staff time and public expense. The people who are the most critical often fail to realize that the expense usually represents a very small portion of the local school budget. The recommendation for this problem is that the State Department of Special Education help the local school system to deal with cases that may generate undue hardship or adverse publicity for Chapter 766.

B. THE EFFECT ON THE PROVISION OF SPECIAL EDUCATION IN THE LEAST RESTRICTIVE APPROPRIATE SETTING. The Gallup survey found that a majority of all education groups thought that special needs children should be educated in the least restrictive environment, with a higher percentage in agreement at the elementary level than at the secondary level. However, most local educators predicted that an increase in class size would be the result of Proposition 2½, which would, in turn, mean more referrals for the more difficult children into more restrictive environments. On the other hand, children returned from private placements, in order to cut costs, will require placement. Therefore, despite the acceptance of the least restrictive environment concept, financial considerations will be a factor in placement decisions. Administrators were observed in some cases to be placing increased pressure to recommend less costly placements.

The recommendation proposed was that the Division of Special Education use the data system developed in the course of this study to help regional staff to monitor significant changes in enrollment in specific program types that might be influenced by budget constraint. A second recommendation was that there be greater cooperation between school systems and collaboratives to identify and develop appropriate programs for students currently in private school placements.

C. THE EFFECTS ON THE DEVELOPMENT OF THE INDIVIDUAL EDUCATION PLAN. The process by which the IEP is developed has given the school staff a useful perspective for understanding the special needs of students and providing appropriate services for them. The formal meetings require teachers, consultants, chairpersons, parents, counselors, and other involved persons to allocate time and meet for the purpose of focusing on the needs of a particular student. It was noted that education plans sometimes were completed with so much specific detail that they were both unrealistic and superfluous in some cases to the local special education staff. Recommendations were made to make the IEP more practical. Also, it was recommended that the IEP, and other student data necessary for staff working with a child, be placed in an accessible place. The report noted that parents needed to take a more active role in the IEP process.

D. THE EFFECTS ON SECONDARY EDUCATION. The number of secondary students receiving special education doubled in the period 1974-1978 and a wider spectrum of programs and services are now available to them. Programs include resource rooms, transition programs, alternative high school programs, and occupational education programs.

Occupational education has received top priority since 1976, especially since admissions to many regional vocational schools are selective and still seem to exclude some students who are in special education. In some cases, alternative high schools are apt to become a dumping ground for all the problems that a local high school has. Despite progress, secondary education is an area where much more progress needs to be made. There are many gaps in services. Some of the new vocational programs are narrow in scope and some students have no access to vocational training.

Recommendations are that local school systems organize interdepartmental task forces at the high school level to consider changes necessary to improve the quality of education for special education children. The Department of Education at the state level should fund more programs organized on the principle of individualizing instruction for all students. The Department of Education should also disseminate information indicating factors that lead to success or failure in various programs. Finally, the Department of Education should develop guidelines detailing what its expectations are for appropriate transition planning from self-contained classrooms to jobs, sheltered workshops or institutions.

E. EFFECTS OF FISCAL FUNDING ISSUES. The total school system expenditure for the implementation of Chapter 766 since its inception is:

1974-75	$143,566,970
1975-76	170,878,210
1976-77	181,414,710
1977-78	211,202,900
1978-79	243,262,827
1979-80	267,741,281

The findings for the financial issues were derived, for the most part, from the Hudson Institute Coordination Case Study. However, some of the data is based on small samples of five non-save-harmless communities. Communities with low property valuation and low per pupil exenditure will find that state aid defrays most of the cost of special education. But Boston, though its property valuation is low, does not benefit from state aid to the same extent as other urban sites because Boston has high per pupil expenditures.

Other important aspects show that:

1. Local administrators do not manipulate special education placement to maximize revenues, including federal revenues.
2. In general, revenues raised through local taxes to support education in Massachusetts have remained relatively constant since 1978.
3. Federal funds for P.L. 94-142 are the most flexible part of the special education budget. School systems can develop new programs, improvement management of special education, train staff, and redesign existing programs.
4. While dramatic increases occurred primarily prior to 1979, funding for private day-care schools and substantially separate programs has continued to increase.
5. In preparing education budgets, there is seldom any understanding of the cost to the community of any expenditures or line items where state aid reimburses most of the cost of Chapter 766. School administrators, especially principals, do not always understand reimbursement processes.

The report stated further that while state aid for special education from 1973 to 1979 increased dramatically, state support of general education did not increase substantially, increased aid for special education did not increase substantially, increased aid for special education was made available by reducing the general aid available through Chapter 70 funds for general education, and state appropriations did not keep pace with rapidly escalating costs for special education.

The recommendations were that:

1. The Department of Education work to see that Chapter 70 ensures adequate funding of the real costs of special education.
2. The Department make clear explanations of financial issues related to special education available to concerned administrators.
3. The legislature should fully fund the bilingual and special education transportation provisions under Chapter 367.
4. The Department of Education should shift to the Department of Mental Health the function of providing for funding for transportation of handicapped adults who are under their jurisdiction.

REFERENCES

Briefing Paper: Initial Review of Regulations Under Part B of the Education of the Handicapped Act, As Amended. U.S. Department of Education. Washington, D.C. 1981.

Commonwealth of Massachusetts, Chapter 766 of the Acts of 1972, The Comprehensive Special Education Law, 1972.

Disparities still exist in who gets special education. U.S. General Accounting Office. Gaithersburg, MD, 1981.

Implementing Massachusetts Special Education Law: A Statewide Assessment. Massachusetts Department of Education. April, 1982.

The Education for All Handicapped Children Act, P.L. No. 94-142, 20, U.S.C. 1401 et seq.

The Rehabilitation Act of 1973, P.L. No. 93-112, 29 U.S.C. 794.

Unanswered questions on educating handicapped children in local public schools. U.S. General Accounting Office. Gaithersburg, MD, 1981.

CHAPTER 3

MINIMUM COMPETENCY TESTING:
WHAT DOES IT MEAN
FOR THE HANDICAPPED?

Introduction

MANY people feel that our public schools are failing. They point to declining test scores, social promotion, education malpractice suits, media publicity, national reports, etc. Schools are perceived as failing and this is intolerable. As a result, increasing demands for accountability in public schools has become a major concern of education today.

The solution to this problem appears to be the requirement of minimum competency testing (MCT) of students. The implication seems to be that public schools were once competent but are currently faltering and that MCT will restore lost competence.

This chapter will focus on three broad issues: first, a general discussion of MCT will be presented; second, a more specific discussion of how MCT impacts on handicapped students; and third, a decisionmaking model will be presented. The model will explore some issues in deciding whether or not to use MCT with handicapped students.

MCT: General

Tests of minimum competency are not a new invention; they

have existed for years in the professions of medicine, law, dentistry, and accounting (Ebel, 1978). The general application of the concept to education is, however, a fairly recent phenomenon. Denver, Colorado appears to have been one of the earliest prototypes for minimum competency testing in education. In 1958, a public opinion survey of 400 business and industrial employers revealed that the validity of the high school diploma was in question. In 1959, the Proficiency and Review Tests were developed in cooperation with the California Test Bureau. In 1960, these tests were administered to seniors — some of whom failed one or more parts (Beal, 1978). Statewide adoption of the MCT concept in California, Florida, and Oregon began in 1975 and 1976 (Pipho, 1978). Today, 39 states have required some type of MCT program (Madaus, 1981).

Minimum competency testing is a response to public perception that schools are failing. The public believes that schools have certified incompetents as competent by passing them along, graduating them, giving them diplomas, and even awarding them college degrees (Ebel, 1978). Sixty-five percent of those surveyed in the 1976 Gallup Poll of the Public's Attitude Towards the Public Schools felt that schools should devote more attention to basic skills. They also said that all high school students in the United States should be required to pass a standard nationwide exam in order to get a high school diploma (Hart, 1978).

Demands for competency testing have been led or pushed by non-educators (Pipho, 1978). The demands come from the public and from legislators speaking for the public (Ebel, 1978). Today, higher standards for grade promotion and high school graduation are second only to lower property taxes as an election year issue in state politics (Pipho, 1978).

According to Madaus (1981), six specific factors led to demands for competency testing in education: 1. decline in SAT scores, 2. employer complaints about lack of basic skills in recent high school graduates, 3. publicity (the Coleman Report) suggests that schools are not effective, 4. education malpractice suits, 5. social promotion, and 6. the accountability movement in education.

Decline in educational achievement in recent decades has occurred. College admission test scores, National Assessment of Educational Progress test results, and norms of standardized tests of school achievement all confirm the impression of professors, parents, and teachers that students are learning less (Ebel, 1978). The implication is that competency testing will help to reverse the decline in test scores. However, this assumption may be invalid for several reasons. First, recent studies (Farr, 1981) have shown that basic skills are improving, especially with younger children and minorities. Many people seem to be confusing basic skills, which are improving, with complex skills, as measured by the SATs and which are declining (Madaus, 1981). Second, students who fail competency tests would probably never take SATs anyway (Madaus, 1981). Third, low academic achievement is not a political problem that can be solved by legislating competency testing; it is a technical problem that requires more knowledge about teaching and learning (Wise, 1978).

Employers have complained about lack of basic skills in recent high school graduates. The impetus for the installation of the Proficiency and Review program in Denver was the 1958 survey of 400 business and industrial employers (Beal, 1978). Ebel (1978) said that demands for competency testing came from disappointed employers. Madaus (1981) however cited a lack of research studies that support this allegation.

There can be no doubt about the flood of adverse publicity (e.g. the Coleman Report) regarding the effectiveness of public schools. For fifteen years, since the appearance of the original Coleman Report in 1966, educators have been reminded repeatedly that "schools do not make a difference" and that family background heavily determines educational achievement. The new Coleman Report dramatically reverses this pessimistic conclusion and finds instead that schools do make a difference, regardless of the family background of students (Ravitch, 1981).

While state legislatures have led the competency testing movement, the federal government has reinforced it, but the judiciary has also participated. The judicial version is known as "education malpractice" (Wise, 1978).

The first widely recognized case of educational malpractice was *Peter Doe* v. *San Francisco Unified School District*. In this case, the plaintiff contended that the school district "failed" to apprehend (Doe's) reading disability and permitted him to graduate from high school, although he was unable to read above the eighth-grade level. The plaintiff argued that he has not achieved a level of minimum competency in reading and that the school was to blame. While "Peter Doe" lost his case, others will follow, and, if the state has a minimum competency testing law in operation, it will be easy to argue that the law makes specific promises concerning what a student will learn (Wise, 1978). A second case, *Robinson* v. *Cahill*, in New Jersey resulted in a court ruling to institute minimum competency testing (Wise, 1978).

While none of the various "education malpractice" suits has yet been resolved in favor of plaintiffs, the widespread implementation of MCT may reverse this trend.

Social promotion assumes that some students are promoted from grade to grade on the basis of age and not academic competence. While this may be true, it is also important to recognize that grade retention currently costs 825 million dollars per year and MCT will only serve to increase numbers of students and expenses in this area (Madaus, 1981).

The final factor involves the accountability movement in education. The Cooperative Accountability Project reported that between 1963 and 1974 at least 73 accountability laws were passed. According to Wise (1978), management ideology has focused concern upon the output of the educational system. That concern has been manifested in two ways: first, numerous systems involving results (CBE, PBE, CBTE, CBTC) have been devised; second, rubrics for minimum expectations for school outcomes have been devised. This translates into the belief that teachers, administrators and school systems should be judged on the basis of student progress and achievement (Madaus, 1981).

Cawelti (1978) reported that the advisory panel on the Scholastic Aptitude Test Score Decline offered the following as possible reasons for declining test scores: demographic changes in the population, television, permissiveness in the family, womens' liberation, higher divorce rates, the decline of religion, the civil rights movement, court decisions, increasing federal regulations, forced busing, and a general crisis in values.

According to Madaus (1981), there are basically four variations in competency testing used by the various states:

1. A single state-mandated test given in grade eleven which determines a student's eligibility for a diploma or a certificate of attendance.
2. Each individual school district may decide to either:
   a. use a state-developed test
   b. develop its own test
   (Illinois and California have adopted this model.)
3. A state MCT may exist and be utilized but not for punitive action. For example, Kansas currently has the best MCT program in the country but only uses the results as information on student progress (Madaus, 1981).
4. New Jersey stands alone. They currently have the most punitive MCT program in the country. For example, student performance on competency tests may be used to fire tenured teachers (Madaus, 1981).

The greatest problem with minimum competency testing is when the tests are used for punitive purposes. Minimum competency tests have been used to deny students a high school diploma, to classify and group students for remediation, and to retain students in grade. When they are used in this manner, as Madaus (1981) says, we are really talking about "incompetency testing."

In addition to the danger cited previously, MCT has other problems:

1. How is "minimum" defined?
2. What kind of competency should we measure?
3. Can one test be used for all students?

The determination of a passing score on a MCT is arbitrary. Depending on which cut score method is used, the percent of students who fail the test can vary dramatically. Will you set one minimum for all students or will you consider ability, special talents, family background, or other factors we know affect the learning of students (Brickell, 1978)? Will you set one minimum for all schools or will you consider community characteristics, faculty composition, school spending, or other factors we know affect the quality of schools (Brickell, 1978)? Minimum is difficult to define and determine.

Competency tests are designed to measure competencies, but what competencies should be measured? The two basic options are school skills or life skills. There is a difference and there are different tests for them (Brickell, 1978). The implication here seems to be that school skills (how to diagram a sentence) may be essentially unrelated to life skills (reading and understanding public signs).

The test itself also presents problems. It would seem that no single test can possibly be fair to all students. This is especially true for handicapped students. Furthermore, the content validity of competency tests has been questioned. The Florida court in the *Debra P.* case found that the state's MCT in fact did not have content validity.

In addition to the problems mentioned, other questions about minimum competency testing should be raised. Will MCTs help or hurt students? Research data from Florida, Virginia, and North Carolina show that blacks and the handicapped will be seriously adversely affected by competency testing. Will MCTs increase student dropouts? Data from Florida shows that during the first year of MCT, the dropout rate increased by 14,000. When MCT was stopped, the dropout rate decreased by 13,000 (Madaus, 1981). What will happen to incompetent students? Give them more chances? Lower standards? Remediate so they can pass? Promote or graduate with a restricted diploma (Brickell, 1978)? What will happen to incompetent schools? Lower standards so they can operate? Refuse to let them operate unless they meet the standard? Let them operate but refuse to accredit them (Brickell, 1978)?

No group is potentially more in conflict with minimum competency testing than the handicapped. The next section of this chapter will explore this special problem.

MCT: The Handicapped

The impetus for the minimum competency testing movement evolved from society's outrage at increasing school costs, declining test scores, and loss of credibility for the high school diploma (Frahm and Covington, 1979; Pipho, 1979). Society is asserting its right to hold school systems accountable through minimum competency testing (Olsen, 1980).

The mandate for MCT extends beyond the "normal" child and includes the handicapped in many states. While MCT proponents argue that it will result in increased literacy for all (McDonald,

1978), such testing raises a number of serious questions and concerns for handicapped students. The basic question is whether MCT mandated for non-handicapped students should also apply to the handicapped. Another question is whether or not the handicapped were considered as states put MCT requirements into effect. It appears that in the scramble to set up MCT programs in response to societal pressure, the handicapped were largely ignored (NASDE, 1979; Pipho, 1979).

According to McCarthy (1980), the following issues must be addressed in dealing with the problem of MCT and the handicapped.

1. Can successful completion of an IEP be used in lieu of an MCT as a high school graduation requirement for a handicapped student?
2. Should some categories of handicapped children be excused from taking MCT?
3. If a handicapped student fails the MCT but successfully completes the IEP, can he/she participate in the graduation ceremony?
4. Can schools issue handicapped students certificates of completion rather than diplomas if they do not take or fail the MCT?
5. If handicapped students receive diplomas without taking the MCT, can non-handicapped students who fail the MCT and do not receive a diploma sue?
6. Can a handicapped student be promoted if he/she achieves the IEP goals but fails the MCT?
7. What technical issues should be addressed in the application of MCT to handicapped populations (e.g. test validity and reliability)?
8. How should the MCT be adapted for the handicapped so that the testing situation will be as fair as possible?
9. What are appropriate qualifications for persons administering and interpreting MCT given to handicapped children?

McClung and Pullin (1978) have identified still other concerns:

1. the potential for racial discrimination
2. inadequate advance notice and phase-in periods prior to the initial use of the tests
3. inadequate match between the instructional program and the

test
4. inadequate remedial instruction that creates or reinforces tracking
5. unfair apportionment of responsibility for test failures between students and educators

Rosewater (1980) says that to the extent that MCT programs fall within the scope of federal regulations (P.L. 94-142, Sec. 504), several standards apply:

1. MCTs must minimize racial and cultural bias.
2. MCT programs must involve standardized administration of valid tests.
3. MCTs must assess specific areas of educational need.

All handicapped children are entitled to a free, appropriate public education in the least restrictive environment. To this end, both P.L. 94-142 and P.L. 93-112 (Sec. 504) were enacted. One important component of the federal legislation is the assumption that each handicapped student requires an individualized education program specifically suited to meet his unique needs. MCT programs, on the contrary, assume that all children should master certain basic skills at a specific time in their school career. Therefore, the federal regulations speak to individualization and divergence, whereas the MCT speaks to group conformity and convergence. It would appear that the use of MCT with handicapped students is inconsistent with the intent of federal regulations. In addition to problems with federal regulations, the use of MCT with the handicapped may also violate state statutes and regulations, as well as the Due Process and Equal Protection Clauses of the Fourteenth Amendment (Rosewater, 1980).

The use of MCT with handicapped students may violate federal regulations. However, mandated exemption of the handicapped also raises serious legal questions. Section 504 of the Rehabilitation Act of 1973 prohibits handicapped students from being denied the opportunity to participate in activities available to non-handicapped students (Rosewater, 1979). Therefore, blanket exemption of the handicapped from MCT seems to pose as many legal problems as does inclusion of the handicapped in MCT programs. This problem is further complicated by the question of how the MCT information will be used. Two options seem possible:

1. MCT data may be used in a positive, constructive way for students. Ravitch (1978) suggested that the ultimate purpose of MCT is to provide assistance to teachers and students rather than to withhold diplomas, but often the tests are administered too late in the student's career to be of much use to him.
2. MCT data may be used punitively. The MCT may be used to deny a high school diploma, to retain a student in grade, or to place a student in a restrictive educational track.

Linde and Olsen (1980) also suggest that MCT programs may be used for two purposes: formative evaluation and summative evaluation. Formative evaluation, designed to make ongoing changes in a program, seems more compatible with the positive approach to MCT. It would appear that this type of approach would be the most beneficial to handicapped children. Summative evaluation, designed to measure final outcomes of a project or process, implies the kind of program potentially punitive to handicapped students. The following diagram (Linde and Olsen, 1980) visually depicts the two options just presented.

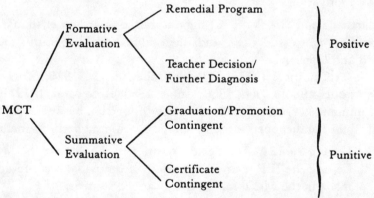

If a handicapped student fails the MCT, two new problems arise, namely, does a remediation program exist and can the student re-take the test? Rosewater (1979) suggests that in many states the answer is yes. However, she also reported that no states surveyed provided remediation and re-testing specifically for handicapped students. Rosewater also suggests that if a handicapped student fails the MCT, he/she should be re-examined and the IEP should be amended. Remediation and re-examination seem to be reasonable expectations if a handicapped student fails the MCT. This would reflect a positive approach to MCT and the handicapped student.

However, many authors have expressed serious concern about the punitive uses of MCT. Perhaps the most serious consequence for the handicapped student concerns diploma denial contingent on failure to pass a competency test. Cohen, Safran, and Polloway (1980) have identified a number of concerns relative to MCT and diploma denial:

1. Failure to pass the MCT may result in the student receiving a certificate of attendance. This may serve to extend the adverse effects of a handicapped label beyond school.
2. MCT is poorly matched to special education curricula. Is it legal to test a student in a novel manner, on new material and, on the basis of such an exam deny a high school diploma?
3. Is the MCT relevant for adult success? Haney and Madaus (1978) questioned whether minimum competencies refer to life skills, survival skills, or academic skills.
4. MCTs may have a detrimental effect on teacher attitude and motivation.

Courtnage and Struck (1978) suggest that to award other than a regular diploma to students brands their educational program substandard and inferior.

Several authors (Masde, 1979; Cohen et al., 1980; Ross and Weintraub, 1980; Olsen, 1980; Amos, 1980; Rosewater, 1979) have recommended establishment of a close connection between IEP and MCT for handicapped students. Some specific suggestions include:

1. Letting the IEP team decide if a student should take the MCT.
2. Letting the IEP team decide what accommodations should be made in the MCT for the handicapped student.
3. Pairing grade promotion and high school diploma on a student's achievement of IEP goals rather than on a score on the MCT.

Olsen (1980) argues that the rationale behind MCT and IEP are similar for the following reasons:

1. The purposes for IEP and MCT are similar: to increase the number of persons who can successfully cope with society.

2. The competencies, although not adequately articulated, are similar.
3. The programs both stress individualization and basic skills.

He also strongly recommends joint planning in the IEP and MCT process among testing and evaluation personnel, special education administrators, teachers, and advocacy groups.

Pullin (1981) has also stated that MCT may work together with IEP requirements to improve educational services to the handicapped.

Rosewater (1979) has suggested that:

1. The IEP development process be used to determine if a handicapped student should take the MCT and what adjustments may be necessary.
2. The requirements of the IEP itself may serve as an alternative standard for promotion or non-promotion if the handicapped student does not participate in the MCT.

Morrissey (1978) suggested a variety of options for handicapped students relative to MCT. One of these was to exempt them from MCT and to use the IEP. Morrissey (1978) also suggested two other options for dealing with MCT and the handicapped. First, the use of different criteria for the handicapped. Specifically, tolerance of lower scores on the MCT or use of teacher ratings and student grades in lieu of MCT. Second, the use of procedural modifications. Specifically, environmental adaptations, format modifications, performance adjustments, and pacing flexibility.

Amos (1980) suggested the following MCT adaptations for the handicapped:

1. Submit the MCT to the IEP committee and let them select the test items for the student.
2. Allow the IEP committee to choose a test that will best evaluate the child's mastery of basic skills.
3. Allow the IEP committee to develop a comparable MCT.

Grise (1980) suggested the following as possible MCT modifications for handicapped students:

1. flexible scheduling
2. flexible setting
3. recording of answers

4. mechanical aids
5. revised format
   a. visual reading
   b. tactile reading
   c. sign language
   d. auditory presentation

MCT: Advantages and Disadvantages

Cohen et al. (1980) have suggested that the following advantages may accompany the use of MCT with handicapped students:

1. Standards for progress and curriculum development will be established.
2. MCT may encourage an increase in achievement motivation.
3. The impact of the exceptional label may be reduced for students who pass the MCT.
4. Early problem identification may be facilitated through periodic competency testing.

Grise (1980) reported that the Council for Administrators of Special Education, Inc., recently and unanimously proposed a resolution to endorse the participation of handicapped students in MCT programs as a logical extension of the concept of mainstreaming.

Cohen et al. (1980) have also identified the following as potential disadvantages in using MCT with handicapped students:

1. MCT may result in handicapped students receiving certificates of attendance in lieu of high school diplomas.
2. A significant discrepancy may exist between the teaching method and MCT for handicapped students.
3. Discriminatory homogeneous remedial grouping of handicapped students may result if they fail MCTs.
4. MCT emphasis on groups may conflict with individual requirements of the IEP.
5. As yet, the relevance of MCT for adult success is unproven.
6. MCT programs may result in an increase of educational barriers for handicapped students.
7. Remedial programs for students who fail the MCT may be of limited value.
8. MCT may have a detrimental effect on teacher attitude and

motivation.

Olsen (1980) has suggested the following reasons for opposing the use of MCT with handicapped students:

1. Inadequate instrumentation exists for measuring competence.
2. The IEP is better able to determine specific competence.
3. The MCT process is unfair to minorities and the handicapped.

Unanswered Questions:

1. Does the MCT program work?
2. Can MCTs be legally mandated for handicapped students?
3. If a student is placed outside an LEA, is he/she still eligible to take an MCT?
4. Should MCTs be used positively or punitively?
5. Can MCTs be modified procedurally for the handicapped while maintaining their validity?
6. What should MCTs measure?
   a. Academic skills?
   b. Vocational skills
   c. Survival skills?

Summary

Minimum competency testing has arisen as a societal response to concern about the quality of public education. Decline in standardized test scores, questionable value of the high school diploma, social promotion, etc., have contributed to this concern. While the arguments for and against MCT continue, its disadvantages are nowhere more apparent than in its application to the handicapped. In spite of all the problems identified previously, it appears that MCTs will continue to be used with handicapped students. Moreover, its use will probably increase.

Proposal

Since MCT programs are currently in effect in thirty-nine states, it is probably safe to assume that they are being applied to handicapped as well as non-handicapped students.

I am proposing that a decisionmaking model be used to decide if a handicapped student should or should not be required to take the

MCT. The model, similar to one from Liberman (1980), proposes four categories and a variety of factors. The categories are (1) for the use of MCT, (2) against the use of MCT, (3) undecided (evidence is equivocal), and (4) not applicable.

Child Factors

TYPE OF HANDICAPPING CONDITION. Children who are visually handicapped or who suffer from cerebral palsy would require, at least, some type of modified MCT. Ultimately, this would have to be looked at on a case-by-case basis.

SEVERITY OF HANDICAPPING CONDITION. Severely handicapped students, especially those severely intellectually handicapped, would probably have little or no chance of passing on MCT. Possible options might include exemption, modified MCT, etc.

STUDENTS IEP. Does the IEP specify whether the student should take the MCT? Can successful completion of the IEP substitute for the MCT?

NOTICE. Has there been sufficient time between notice that MCT would be given and the actual test date?

School Factors

Why is the MCT used? If it is used punitively, the consequences would seem to be more serious than if it is non-punitive.

Is the MCT tied to diploma denial? What if the handicapped student fails the MCT but achieves all goals in the IEP?

Is the MCT tied to grade promotion? Should the student's promotion be based on MCT, IEP, or other factors?

Is the MCT tied to tracking? Is it legal to track handicapped students who fail MCT? Would such tracking violate the least restrictive alternative requirement of P.L. 94-142?

Is a remedial program available? If a handicapped student fails the MCT, should he be placed in a remedial program?

How would this conflict with special education programming and the IEP requirements?

What is the match between MCT and instruction? Is there a direct connection between the MCT and special education instruction for the handicapped student?

	For MCT	Against MCT	Undecided	Does Not Apply
CHILD FACTORS				
Type of handicap				
Severity of handicap				
IEP and MCT				
Notice				
SCHOOL FACTORS				
Why is MCT used				
MCT and diploma denial				
MCT and grade promotion				
MCT and tracking				
MCT and remediation				
MCT and instruction				
MCT FACTORS				
Who administers and interprets the MCT				
What does the test measure				
Reliability and MCT				
Validity and MCT				
Standardization				
Accommodations possible				

Minimum Competency Test Factors

Who administers and interprets the test? Is the MCT administered and interpreted by a licensed psychometrist?

What does the test purport to measure? Does the test measure
academic skills, life survival skills, etc.?

Is the test reliable? Is any reliability data on the MCT for handicapped students available?

Is the test valid? Is validity data on the MCT for handicapped
students available?

Has the test been standardized with handicapped students? Has
the MCT been standardized? Were any handicapped students included in the standardization sample?

Are any accommodations to be used? Can the MCT be modified
for handicapped students? If the MCT is modified, does it retain validity and reliability?

REFERENCES

Amos, K.M.: Competency testing: will the LD student be included? *Exceptional Children, 47*(3):194-197, 1980.

Beal, B.B.: Denver, Colorado: A 17-year-old MCT program. *Phi Delta Kappan, 59*(9):610-611, 1978.

Brickell, H.M.: Seven key notes on minimum competency testing. *Phi Delta Kappan, 59*(9):589-592, 1978.

Cawelti, C.: National competency testing: a bogus solution. *Phi Delta Kappan, 58*(9):619-621, 1978.

Cohen, S.B., Safran, J., and Polloway, E.: Minimum competency testing: implications for mildly retarded students. *Education and Training of the Mentally Retarded*, 1980, pp. 250-255.

Competency Testing, Special Education and the Awarding of Diplomas: A report
of survey information. National Association of State Directors of Special
Education and the North Carolina Department of Public Instruction, Division of Exceptional Children. Washington, D.C., February, 1979.

Cooperative Accountability Project, Legislation by the States: Accountability
and Assessment in Education, Report No. 2, Denver, Colorado: CAP, 1974,
p. 7.

Courtnage, L., and Struck, J.: Rights of retarded people to receive regular diplomas and participate in high school graduation exercises. *Mental Retardation,
16*:58-59, 1978.

Ebel, R.L.: The case for minimum competency testing. *Phi Delta Kappan,*

59(8):546-549, 1978.

Farr, R.: Three National Assessments of Reading: Changes in Performance, 1970-80, Report No. 11-R-01. Education Commission of the States, Suite 700, 1860 Lincoln Street, Denver, Colorado 80295, April, 1981.

Frahm, R., and Covington, J.: *What's happening in minimum competency testing? Phi Delta Kappan*, Bloomington, IN., 1979.

Grise, P.: Florida's minimum competency testing program for handicapped students. *Exceptional Children, 47*(3):186-191, 1980.

Hart, G.S.: The California pupil proficiency law as viewed by its author. *Phi Delta Kappan, 59*(8):592-595, 1978.

Lieverman, L.M.: A decision-making model for in-grade retention (nonpromotion). *Journal of Learning Disabilities, 13*(5):268-272, 1980.

Linde, J., and Olsen, K.: *Minimum Competency Testing and Handicapped Students*. Lexington, KY: Mid-South Regional Resource Center, 1980.

Madaus, G.: "Minimum Competency Testing and Handicapped Students." Speech delivered at Boston College, June 1, 1981.

McCarthy, M.: Minimum competency testing and handicapped students. *Exceptional Children, 47*(3):166-173, 1980.

McClung, M., and Pullin, D.: Competency testing and handicapped students. *Clearinghouse Review, 11*:922-927, 1978.

McDonald, T.F.: Pro:minimal competency testing as viewed from the front line. *Journal of Reading, 22*:13-14, 1978.

Morrissey, P.: Adaptive testing: "How and When Should Handicapped Students be Accommodated in Competency Testing Programs." Paper presented at the American Educational Research Association Topical Conference on Competency Achievement Testing, Washington, D.C., October 13, 1978.

Olsen, K.R.: Minimum competency testing and the IEP process. *Exceptional Children, 47*(3):176-183, 1980.

Pipho, C.: Minimum competency testing in 1978 — A look at state standards. *Phi Delta Kappan, 59*(9):585-588, 1978.

Pullin, D.: *Mandated Minimum Competency Testing: Its Impact on Handicapped Adolescents*. Cambridge, MA: Center for Law and Education, 1981.

Ravitch, D.: The meaning of the new Coleman Report. *Phi Delta Kappan, 62*(10):718-720, 1981.

Rosewater, A.: *Minimum Competency Testing Programs and Handicapped Students: Perspectives on Policy and Practice*. Washington, D.C.: Institute for Educational Leadership, 1979.

Ross, J.W., and Weintraub, F.J.: Policy approaches regarding the impact of graduation requirements on handicapped students. *Exceptional Children, 47*(3):200-203, 1980.

Wise, A.E.: Minimum competency testing: Another case of hyperrationalization. *Phi Delta Kappan, 59*(3):596-598, 1978.

CHAPTER 4

EXTENDED SCHOOL YEAR:
IS IT REQUIRED BY P.L. 94-142?

MANY of the educational controversies discussed in this book have arisen as a result of efforts to define the "appropriate" education to which handicapped children are entitled under P.L. 94-142. One of the most popular controversies concerns extended school year (ESY), or schooling past 180 days. The basic question here is whether an appropriate education for all handicapped children, especially the severely and profoundly handicapped, can be provided in the traditional 180-day school year. Stated another way, the issue is whether or not school districts must provide an educational program in excess of 180 days for some handicapped children.

The seminal court case dealing with ESY has been *Armstrong* v. *Kline* (476 F. Supp. 583, 1979). In this case, three related class action suits were combined against the Pennsylvania State Secretary of Education (Caryl Kline), school districts, private schools, and others for violating children's rights by denying them free, publicly supported education in excess of 180 days. According to Stotland and Mancuso (1981), the suit was a cross-category action, covering all types of handicapped youngsters including autistic, severely and profoundly mentally retarded, and severely emotionally disturbed. In this case, a hearing examiner had determined that year-round education was necessary to prevent regression in a student because of his serious handicapping condition. Contrary to the examiner's findings, the Pennsylvania Department of Education issued a policy refusing to fund programs beyond 180 days. In addition, the department also directed all hearing officers who preside at special education due process hearings that they were without the power to order or approve any educational programs exceeding 180 days per year (Stotland and Mancuso, 1981).

Plaintiff's allegations in the case were that:

1. The existing "180-day rule" was a violation of P.L. 94-142's requirement that each handicapped child must receive a free, appropriate public education.
2. The Department of Education was denying handicapped children and their parents their rights to procedural safeguards under P.L. 94-142 by refusing to allow the question of ESY to be the subject of any due process hearing.

In March, 1979, a two-week trial was held in which plaintiffs proved the following (Stotland and Mancuso, 1981).:

1. As a result of their handicaps, plaintiffs learn very slowly, are negatively affected when their educational programs are interrupted, and take a substantial amount of time to regain or recoup these losses once their formal programming resumes.
2. Plaintiffs showed that these same learning characteristics are shared by other handicapped children.
3. Although plaintiffs' impairments may limit their ultimate prognosis and make unlikely the achievement of total self-sufficiency and independence from caretakers, it is unlikely that any real progress towards these goals can be achieved unless the regression/recoupment syndrome caused by the 180-day limitation can be prevented.

On September 5, 1979, Judge Clarence Newcomer issued the following decision: "A handicapped student is entitled to an educational program in excess of 180 days if regression caused by an interruption in educational programming together with a student's limited recoupment capacities renders it impossible or unlikely that the student will attain the level of self sufficiency or independence from caretakers that the student would otherwise be expected to reach in view of his or her handicapping condition."

The court ruled that this standard must be applied to each child on an individual basis. Following the court's decision, defendants appealed to the United States Court of Appeals for the Third Circuit. On July 15, 1980, the Third Circuit Court of Appeals handed down its decision in the case of *Armstrong* v. *Kline* (*Battle* v. *Commonwealth*).

Writing for all three members of the appellate panel, Judge Hunter affirmed the district court's holding that the Pennsylvania Department of Education's 180-day rule violated P.L. 94-142 (Stotland and Mancuso, 1981). In summary, then, plaintiffs succeeded in obtaining a favorable ruling on all issues raised in the original complaint. The 180-day rule was declared illegal and the key argument of plaintiffs endorsed; namely, that to be appropriate a special education program must be based on an individual assessment and an individual planning process, which must result in an individualized program designed to meet each child's unique needs. Any absolute rule applied without exception to all handicapped children cannot coexist with this mandate (Stotland and Mancuso, 1981). Just as PARC provided the impetus for numerous right-to-education cases, so also has Armstrong instigated numerous ESY cases. According to a report issued by the Education Advocate Coalition on Federal Compliance, litigation or administrative proceedings dealing with extended school year are currently pending in Oregon, Georgia, Texas, Michigan, Ohio, Mississippi, and South Carolina. In addition, litigation is contemplated in California. Children in Virginia, Maine, the District of Columbia, Maryland, Illinois, Nebraska, and Oklahoma have reported difficulty in obtaining needed services in excess of 180 days.

According to *Student Litigation* by Marvel, Galfo, and Rockwell, forty-six ESY cases were litigated between 1977 and 1981. For summaries and references to the specific cases, the reader is referred to this publication.

Having discussed the *Armstrong* case in some detail procedurally, I would now like to explore some of the salient issues that influenced the court's decision. A thorough and well-documented summary of these issues was presented by Leonard (1981). The following section presents a brief summary of these major points:

1. loss of skills due to interruptions in programming
2. factors reducing efficacy of the education system

3. maximizing instructional time for SPI children

1. Loss of Skills Due to Interruptions in Programming

Expert witnesses who testified for plaintiffs and defendants in the *Armstrong* case agreed that SPI and SED children experience a significant loss of skills during substantial interruptions in educational programming. However, they disagreed about what brought about this skill loss.

Defendants offered the following explanations as possible reasons for student regression:

a. The loss is merely coincidental with breaks in programming.
b. The loss is due to a lack of education in functional skills.
c. The loss is due to teacher incompetence.
d. The loss is due to parents' failure to maintain children's programming.

Plaintiffs alleged that the loss of skills was due to the absence of programming. The court upheld the plaintiffs' argument.

2. Factors Reducing Efficacy of the Education System

a. The need for relearning each year after summer breaks.
b. The inability to rely on the year-end assessment conducted by previous teachers.
c. The greater costs of residential settings necessitated by the handicapped individual's inability to live in the community because of unavailability of summer programming or the lack of attainment by age 21 of skills necessary for living in a community residence.
d. The loss of family and community contribution to the education and development of a person who, because there is no summer program, must be institutionalized at a great distance rather than remain in a group home.
e. The loss of the ability to maximize the most critical times for learning.

3. Maximizing Instructional Time

A recent study by Fredericks et al. (1978) found that the most important factor in determining progress made by severely handicapped students was the number of minutes of instruction per day. Another study (McCormick and Goldman, 1979) found, however, that severely handicapped students receive less instruction than children in higher functioning disability areas because of time consumed by caretaking.

In summary, it appears that SPI students need more instructional time than other handicapped students but they get less. Therefore, any interruptions in programming probably have a more serious effect on them than it would on other handicapped children.

Based on existing case law, it appears that rigid adherence to the 180-day school rule may be a violation of P.L. 94-142, especially for SPI and SED children.

Given the clarity of the court's decision in *Armstrong* and the subsequent plethora of litigation regarding ESY, it is surprising that the United States Department of Education has failed to issue a clear policy statement regarding extended school year.

On the other hand, the United States Office for Civil Rights issued a policy interpretation on January 18, 1980, pursuant to Section 504 of the Rehabilitation Act of 1973, requiring school districts to provide summer programs for handicapped children who need them.

School District Options

It would appear that school districts have two options with regard to ESY:

1. They can obey a clear mandate from the courts to provide schooling past 180 days.
2. They can fight the ESY concept.

In essence, ESY requires that school districts do two things:

1. Identify eligible handicapped children.
2. Develop quality summer programs for identified students.

The issue of "who is eligible for ESY?" is primarily one that local school districts should decide. However, they may look to the court's decision in *Armstrong* for guidance. For example, it would appear that severely and profoundly impaired as well as severely emotionally disturbed children are more likely to need ESY than other handicapped students for reasons cited previously.

Further guidance on eligibility can also be found in Judge Newcomer's decision: "A handicapped student is entitled to...ESY if regression caused by an interruption in educational programming together with...limited recoupment capacities...renders...attainment of...self sufficiency or independence from caretakers...impossible."

Ultimately, the decision here should rest with the IEP team considering each student on an individual basis. Once the school district has determined who is eligible for ESY programs, it must then decide what these programs should do (i.e. what is the purpose of ESY?).

Larsen, Goodman, and Glean (1981) have offered the following ideas about ESY. First, they say, the most important reason for ESY is to prevent skill loss or regression in eligible students. Second, ESY programs may offer opportunities to reinforce learned skills and behavior in varied natural settings and applications. Third, ESY programs can also be used to develop new skills on the part of students participating in them.

Opposition to the ESY concept is not new. Larsen, Goodman, and Glean (1981) reported that many educators, administrators, and professional education organizations are openly opposed to extended school year programs. They cited the request by the National School Boards Association (NSBA) to file an *amicus curiae* brief in *Crawford* v. *Pittman* (1980), an extended school year case under litigation in Mississipi. In responding to the plaintiff's position that some handicapped children need summer programming in order to attain their highest possible level of self-sufficiency, the NSBA argued that public education does not guarantee that any child will reach full potential. Furthermore, NSBA argued that funding summer programs for some handicapped students would seriously reduce financial resources needed to support the education of other handicapped and non-handicapped students. This issue of "full potential" may take on new meaning now in light of the Supreme Court's decision in the *Rowley* case.

Another argument against the ESY concept was articulated by Makuch (1981). He argues that P.L. 94-142 is not the appropriate vehicle for guaranteeing free, appropriate "human" services to all handicapped people and their families.

Makuch also says that the so-called related services are really primary or essential services that must be provided regardless of whether or not they are needed to enable the person to profit from special education. He goes on to suggest that interagency cooperation will be unattainable unless each human service agency is obligated by law to perform equally.

Finally, Makuch suggests that total dependence on the education system will make services unavailable priol to and subsequent to school age.

Summary

The concept of extended school year or schooling past 180 days is controversial. The court, in the *Armstrong* case clearly articulated a standard which said that some handicapped children may require a summer program in order to receive a free, appropriate public education guaranteed by P.L. 94-142.

Eligibility for ESY programs should be made on a case-by-case basis, however, some guidelines do exist. Key variables to consider according to Larsen, Goodman, and Glean (1981) are (1) type of handicapping condition, (2) evidence of a regression-recoupment disability, and (3) the goal of self-sufficiency.

Once eligible students have been identified, school districts must develop appropriate programs. Some key considerations in designing these programs should be skill maintenance, generalization programming, and skill acquisition.

Finally, opposition to such programs has existed and will continue to exist in the future. It will be interesting to see if such opposition increases in light of the recent Supreme Court decision in *Rowley*.

Proposal

Extended school year programs are currently in existence in several states and, in light of court decisions, it is likely that such programs will be increasingly demanded by parents and advocates.

The IEP team will in all likelihood be required to decide which students are eligible to participate in ESY programs. In order to assist IEP teams in this selection process, I am proposing a decision-making model. This model is similar to another one reported elsewhere in this book relative to minimum competency testing. This model also proposes the following categories:

a. for ESY
b. against ESY
c. undecided
d. not applicable

I am also proposing that a variety of factors be considered:

a. student factors
b. home factors
c. school factors

Child Factors

a. type of handicapping condition
b. severity of handicapping condition
c. evidence of regression-recoupment disability
d. the goal of self-sufficiency
e. age

School Factors

a. financial resources
b. space availability
c. transportation
d. availability of trained staff
e. availability of necessary support services (PT, OT, etc.)
f. availability of skill-maintenance programs
g. availability of generalization programs
h. availability of skill-acquisition programs
i. availability of the eligible student

	For ESY	Against ESY	Undecided	Does Not Apply
CHILD FACTORS				
Type of handicap				
Severity of handicap				
Regression—recoupment disability				
Goal of self-sufficiency				
Age				
SCHOOL FACTORS				
Student availability				
Financial resources				
Space				
Transportation				
Staff				
Support services				
Maintenance programs				
Generalization programs				
Acquisition programs				
HOME FACTORS				
Parental approval				
Home programming				

Home Factors
   a. parental approval for ESY
   b. parental expertise to provide summer programming at home
   c. parental time to provide summer programming at home

REFERENCES

Armstrong v. Kline, 476 F. Supp. 583 (E.D. Pa. 1979), Aff'd CA 78-0172 (3rd Cir. July 15, 1980).

Battle v. Commonwealth, 79-2158, 79-2188-90, 79-2568-70 (3rd Cir., July 18, 1980).

Board of Education of The Hendrick Hudson Central School District, Westchester County, et al. v. Rowley.

Crawford v. Pittman, Docket No. GC 8016 WKO (U.S. District Court, North District of Mississippi, Greenville, April 2, 1980).

Fredricks, H.D., Anderson, R., Baldwin, V.L., Grove, D., Moore, W., and Beaird, J.: The identification of competencies of teachers of the severely handicapped. Project report (Grant #OEG - 0 - 74 - 2775). Monmouthe, OR: Teaching Resources Division, Oregon State Agency for Higher Education, 1978.

Larsen, L., Goodman, L., and Glean, R.: Issues in the Implementation of extended school year programs for handicapped students. *Exceptional Children,* 47(4):256-263, 1981.

Leonard, J.: 180-day barrier: issues and concerns, *Exceptional Children,* 47(4):246-253, 1981.

Makuch, G.J.: Year-round special education and related services: a state director's perspective. *Exceptional Children,* 47(4):272-274, 1981.

Marvel, T., Galfo, H., and Rockwell, J.: Student litigation: a compilation and analysis of civil cases involving students, 1977-1981, National Center for State Courts.

McCormick, L., and Goldman, R.: The transdisciplinary model: implications for service delivery and personnel preparation for the severely and profoundly handicapped. *AAESPH Review,* 4(2):152-161, 1979.

Report by the Education Advocates on Federal Compliance Activities to Implement the Education for All Handicapped Children Act (PL 94-142), Education for The Handicapped Law Report. May 1980.

Stotland, J.F., and Mancuso, E.: U.S. court of appeals decision regarding Armstrong v. Kline: The 180-day rule. *Exceptional Children,* 47(4):266-270, 1981.

CHAPTER 5

SUSPENSION/EXPULSION
OF HANDICAPPED STUDENTS:
IS IT LEGAL?

Introduction

THE power of local school authorities to adapt reasonable rules and regulations covering pupil conduct is essential to the efficient functioning of the schools (Reutter & Hamilton, 1970). However, discipline continues to be a significant problem in public education today. For example, a recent Gallup Poll (1982) of the public's attitude towards the public schools reported that "lack of discipline" continues to be the major problem confronting public education. The report also states that in 13 of 14 education polls conducted, discipline has been identified as the major problem in education. Finally, 7 persons in 10 suveyed by the poll reported that discipline was a "very serious" or "fairly serious" problem.

Learning cannot occur in a chaotic environment. Therefore, teachers need the authority to direct students and punish them for infractions the same as parents would. When pupils are under the jurisdiction of the schools, teachers are said to stand *in loco parentis*, i.e. in the place of the parent to the students (Reutter & Hamilton, 1970). Reutter and Hamilton (1970) also point out that the status of the teacher to the child is an essential element in establishing the standard of reasonableness in regard to punishment: Under similar circumstances would it be reasonable for a parent to inflict the punishment?

In summary, schools have the power to adapt reasonable rules governing pupil conduct, and discipline continues to be a serious problem in public education. Wayson and Pinnell (n.d.) suggested that the following techniques are available to schools in order to deal with discipline problems: corporal punishment, expulsion, suspension, security forces, detention, sending students to the principal's office, transfers, loss of privileges, and in-house suspension. In many ways, the most serious of these options available to school authorities is suspension/expulsion of students, since it usually means that for a period of time the student receives no educational program.

In suspension, the student must leave school for a specified period of time. Suspension also requires that the school provide written notice prior to enactment, a written statement of the reasons for this action, and finally an opportunity for an informal hearing. The following advantages make suspension attractive as a disciplinary strategy:

1. The disruptive student is removed.
2. This student cannot disturb others.
3. Parents may be required to come to school for a conference.

However, suspension also has disadvantages:

1. It can teach the student that power is absolute and arbitrary.
2. The student may feel helpless if due process has not happened.
3. It has little positive educational value.
4. It gives students official approval to be out of school.
5. The student often receives no educational program.
6. The student may have no supervision at home and may be "on the streets."

Expulsion is more serious than suspension because it means that the student is out of school for a longer period of time. With expulsion, the student is required to leave school for more than 10 days. Prior to expulsion, schools must provide written notice to the parent, written statements of reasons for the action, notification of opportunity for a hearing, and notice of time and place for the hearing. Expulsion may be said to have the following advantages:

1. Immediate cessation of the problem behavior by removing the disruptive student from school.
2. Can facilitate class atmosphere by removing conduct problem students.
3. Removes the disrupting students before they spread.

However, expulsion also has disadvantages:

1. Students are forced out of school and the presenting problem remains unresolved.
2. Effects are the same as under suspension but more severe.
3. School causes for problem behavior are not addressed.
4. Students usually receive no educational program during the period of expulsion.
5. The student may be unsupervised at home or "on the streets."

According to a report by the National School Resource Network (1980), data on suspension suggest a number of questionable implications about its use as a disciplinary strategy. Advocates for children have pointed out that suspension policies may discriminate against non-white students, and educators are concerned about the loss of valuable class time by poor students who are suspended or expelled. While the issue of suspension/expulsion is serious for the student doing poorly, minority students, and others, its most lethal use may be with handicapped students.

The controversial nature of this topic can be seen in the fact that . . . suspension and expulsion of handicapped students has been selected as a "target of opportunity for deregulation" by the United States Department of Education. The following reasons were cited by the department:

1. Administrators and local school personnel are concerned as to whether handicapped students can or should be treated differently from their non-handicapped peers.
2. Education officials feel that expulsion of handicapped students is not a federal issue but should be treated as part of a school's overall program of discipline and is most appropriately a state and local issue.
3. Administrators identified a need for information in determining the relationship between a student's behavior and handicap

to meet the standards stated in certain court decisions.

4. Commentors have urged the department to clarify that EHA, by its terms, does not permit total or permanent exclusion of a handicapped child from needed special education and related services.

Boundy (1982) points out that the rights of children with special needs to receive a publicly supported education and not to be excluded on the basis of their handicap has been recognized by federal courts on due process and equal protection grounds and on state constitutional and statutory grounds.

Federal law governing services to handicapped students replaces local school board policies regarding discipline of the handicapped. Under the Education of the Handicapped Act (P.L. 94-142) and Section 504 of the Rehabilitation Act handicapped children are entitled to a free, appropriate public education. Any action by a public school that interrupts access to an appropriate education is regulated under these acts, including disciplinary sanctions (Martin, 1981).

The remainder of this chapter will be organized around five specific questions. These are questions that public schools must address prior to disciplining handicapped students via suspension/expulsion.

1. Does suspension/expulsion deny the right of a handicapped student to a free, appropriate public education?

Handicapped students who engage in misbehavior and disciplinary infractions are subject to normal school disciplinary rules and procedures so long as such treatment does not abridge the right to a free appropriate public education (Pullin, 1981). Federal courts have enjoined school districts from expelling or constructively excluding handicapped students for misbehavior when such procedures violate a student's right to a free, appropriate public education. Specific cases include: *Stuart* v. *Nappi, Howard S.* v. *Friendswood Independent School District, Doe* v. *Koger, S-1 Turlington, Doe* v. *Maher, Sherry* v. *New York State Education Department.*

Stuart v. *Nappi* is perhaps the case most frequently cited in the literature dealing with suspension/expulsion. Because of its importance, the specifics of this case will be discussed in some detail. Moreover, the court's decision speaks to the issue of free, appropriate public education.

In this case, the court issued an injunction prohibiting the expulsion of a learning disabled student with a history of disciplinary problems. The court ruled that any non-emergency exclusion, regardless of whether it was for behavior related to the handicapping condition, would deprive a handicapped student of his/her right to an "appropriate education" (Boundy, 1982).

This case deals with the attempted expulsion of a third-year handicapped student at Danbury High School. Kathy Stuart, the plaintiff, was described as having learning disabilities, limited intelligence, and behavior problems. She has been receiving special education services since February, 1975. At this time, a psychological evaluation was requested, but the testing was not done until June, 1976. By late fall, 1976, Kathy stopped attending her special education classes and merely wandered the halls. A team meeting held in March, 1977 recommended continuation of special education classes, but the plaintiff never attended special classes during the 1977-78 school year.

On September 14, 1977, Stuart was involved in a school-wide disturbance. She was subsequently suspended for 10 days and a disciplinary hearing was scheduled for November 30, 1977. At this hearing, the superintendent of schools recommended to the school board that she be expelled for the remainder of the school year. The plaintiff subsequently asked the court to issue a preliminary injunction to prevent her expulsion and it was granted. The court reasoned that expulsion would result in irreparable harm to plaintiff since she would be without the special education to which she was entitled.

The court's decision hinged on four standards found in P.L. 94-142, namely: free, appropriate public education, least restrictive environment, change in placement only in accordance with prescribed procedures, and continuation in present placement while a complaint is pending.

The court clearly did not mean to imply that schools were powerless in disciplining handicapped students. This is evident in the following statement:

> Handicapped children are neither immune from a school's disciplinary process nor are they entitled to participate in programs when their behavior impairs the education of other children in the program. First, school authorities can take swift disciplinary measures, such as suspen-

sion, against disruptive handicapped children. Secondly, a PPT (planning and placement team) can request a change in placement of handicapped children who have demonstrated that their present placement is inappropriate by disrupting the education of other children. The Handicapped Act thereby affords schools with both short-term and long-term methods of dealing with handicapped children who are behavior problems.

Boundy (1982) reports that other federal courts have held that handicapped students may be subject to short-term non-emergency suspensions for up to 10 days without triggering their rights to procedural safeguards under P.L. 94-142. Specific cases include *Stanley* v. *School Administrative Unit No. 40, Milford–Mount Vernon and Board of Education of the City of Peoria* v. *Illinois State Board of Education.*

It appears that schools may suspend handicapped students in certain cases if the following conditions prevail. First, an emergency situation must exist. The *Stuart* court defined an emergency situation as one in which (1) the student is violent and presents an ongoing danger or threat of physical injury to himself/herself or others or where the student's conduct is so disruptive over a lengthy period of time that normal classroom activities cannot possibly continue, and (2) this ongoing threat of injury or disruption cannot be reduced or eliminated by less exclusionary means. Second, the suspension should not exceed 10 days cumulatively or consecutively in a school year. Third, students facing possible suspension are entitled to procedural due process (*Goss* v. *Lopez*). Where an emergency situation justifies a delay in the normal hearing procedures for a suspension, a preliminary hearing must be held as soon as practicable and in no case later than 72 hours after the removal of the student from his/her regular education placement (Boundy, 1982).

The procedure outlined previously was further supported by the court decision in *Mattie T.* v. *Holladay.* The court, in this case, specified that a child may only be removed from a special education program for disciplinary reasons when the child's behavior represents an immediate physical danger to himself/herself or others or constitutes a clear emergency within the school such that removal from school is essential.

In summary, then, the following points emerge:

1. Handicapped students have a statutory right to a free, appropriate public education.

2. Any suspension or expulsion is a deprivation of that right.
3. Suspensions or expulsions should be minimized with handicapped students (less than 10 days) and should only be used when an emergency situation exists.

2. Does suspension/expulsion violate a handicapped student's right to have change in placement occur only through prescribed procedures?

The basic question here seems to be whether or not suspension/expulsion of a handicapped student constitutes a change in educational placement. If it does, then under P.L. 94-142 and Section 504 handicapped students are entitled to certain rights, one of which states that all changes in educational placement must be effectuated in accordance with prescribed procedures. Several recent court decisions have shed light on this question.

A recent decision by the Sixth United States Circuit Court of Appeals, in *Kaelin* v. *Grubbs*, stated that schools must follow federal due process procedures before expelling handicapped students because such disciplinary action is tantamount to changing educational placements.

In *Kenneth* v. *Kline*, the plaintiff was an emotionally disturbed student who was expelled from school for participation in a disruptive incident. The expulsion was not treated as a change in placement, however, plaintiff contended that all suspensions and expulsions should be treated as placement changes. The result was that parties involved in this action entered into an agreement whereby the school district adopted suspension/expulsion procedures.

Similar court decision suggesting that suspension/expulsion is a change in placement can be found in the following cases: *Lopez* v. *Salida School District, Stuart* v. *Nappi, Mrs. A.J.* v. *Special School District No. 1, S-1* v. *Turlington, Doe* v. *Maher, Sherry* v. *New York State Education Department, Doe* v. *Koger,* and *Blue* v. *New Haven Board of Education.*

In summary, the following points have been clarified by the courts (Boundy, 1982):

1. Exclusion beyond 10 days, regardless of the reason, is suffi-

ciently lengthy to amount to a removal from the student's current placement.

2. Such change in educational program requires proper change in placement procedures.
3. These procedures include determination that current placement is no longer least restrictive.
4. A new plan for appropriate education in the least restrictive environment should be formulated.
5. Educational status must be protected pending the proceedings.

3. Does suspension/expulsion abridge a handicapped student's right to be educated in the least restrictive environment?

As far as the *Stuart* court goes, the answer to this question seems to be *yes*. The court points out that an important feature of the handicapped act is its requirement that the children be educated in the least restrictive environment. The court goes on to say that the right to education in the least restrictive environment may be circumvented if schools are permitted to expel handicapped children. An expulsion has the effect of restricting the availability of alternative placements.

Both P.L. 94-142 and Section 504 guarantee the right that handicapped students should be placed in regular classes with non-handicapped students to the maximum extent possible. Furthermore, P.L. 94-142 requires that special classes, separate schooling, or other removal of the handicapped regular classes should only occur when the nature or severity of the handicap is such that education in regular classes with the use of supplementary aids and services cannot be achieved satisfactorily.

The concept of least restrictive environment previously referred to is closely related to the term *mainstreaming*. Mainstreaming is a term of art accruing from the principle of least restrictive environment, a principle which by definition acknowledges the differences between handicapped children and their non-handicapped peers (Pullin, 1981). These differences were often used by public schools to exclude handicapped children from public education. The least restrictive environment (mainstreaming) principle was a critical component of P.L. 94-142 in light of the history of isolation and segregation of handicapped children.

This least restrictive environment principle was again reiterated by the courts in *Hairston* v. *Drosick*. This case involved an attempt by a school district to place a spina bifida child in another school where it would be easier to deal with her physical needs. The court found that this was not sufficiently compelling to warrant her movement to a more restrictive educational setting and they required that she be served in regular classes. The court said that handicapped school children must be educated in regular classes unless there is a compelling educational justification for placement elsewhere. Finally, the court held that exclusion of a handicapped child, except as a last resort, violates the student's rights under both P.L. 94-142 and Section 504.

Other cases in which the courts have relied on the least restrictive environment requirement as a basis for rejecting the use of disciplinary or other exclusionary proceedings against handicapped students include: *Howard S.* v. *Friendswood Independent School District, Blue* v. *New Haven Board of Education, P-1* v. *Shedd, Mattie T.* v. *Holladay,* and *Southeast Warren Community School District* v. *Department of Public Instruction* (Boundy, 1982).

To summarize here, the courts have clearly stated that suspension/expulsion, except in emergency situations, circumvents a handicapped student's right to be educated in the least restrictive environment. This right is guaranteed by both P.L. 94-142 and Section 504.

4. Does suspension/expulsion require a due process hearing for a handicapped student?

Both P.L. 94-142 and Section 504 guarantee the right to an impartial hearing to settle disputes between parents, students, and public schools regarding the free, appropriate education of handicapped students.

According to Pullin (1981), most expulsions and long-term suspensions are determined by the local school board. This, in effect, places the local school board in the position of using a school disciplinary proceeding to determine the existence and nature of a handicapping condition and the appropriate educational placement of the student. Such proceedings appear to undercut the essence of due process protections afforded by the federal laws. These protections include hearings and procedures to afford: "An opportunity to present complaints with respect to any matter relating to the identification, evaluation, or educational placement of the child or the provision of a free appropriate public education to such a child" 20 U.S.C. 1H15 (b) (1) (E). As pointed out previously in this section, the courts have determined that suspension/expulsion constitutes a change in placement for a handicapped student. Therefore, the use of this disciplinary action seems to require that parents and students be afforded the opportunity for a hearing.

Due process hearings for special education matters must be conducted by impartial hearing officers under both P.L. 94-142 and Section 504. The regulations promulgated under P.L. 94-142 define the characteristics of a hearing officer: "A hearing may not be conducted: (1) By a person who is an employee of a public agency which is involved in the education or care of the child, or (2) by any person having a personal or professional interest which would conflict with his or her objectivity in the hearing" 45 C.F.R. 121a 507 (a).

Further clarification of the hearing officer was provided by HEW on August 14, 1978 when it issued an official policy interpretation under Section 504: "School board members may not serve as hearing officers in proceedings conducted to resolve disputes between parents or handicapped children and officials of their school system" 43 Fed Reg. 360.36 (August 14, 1978).

The question of whether school officials may participate in due process hearings has also been addressed in two court cases. The court in both *Campochiaro* v. *Califano* and *Robert M.* v. *Benton* clearly stated that such officials should not participate in due process hearings. In summary, then, the following points emerge: first, if a handicapped student or his/her parent contests an attempted disciplinary exclusion of the student, a complaint under P.L. 94-142 and Section 504 exists and the impartial due process hearing mechanism is triggered; second, the use of local school board members has been found to be inadequate to insure impartiality and to afford handicapped students procedural protections to which they are entitled (Pullin, 1981).

5. Does the public school have a right to suspend/expel a handicapped student if it can show that the alleged misconduct is not related to the student's handicapping condition?

School authorities may not apply suspension policies or other disciplinary sanctions to handicapped students referred for evaluation when the conduct for which the measures are being considered is an element of, or related to, the student's handicap or is the result of an inappropriate educational program or placement. Any such action could be challenged under P.L. 94-142, Section 504, or the Equal Protection and Due Process Clauses of the Fourteenth Amendment (Boundy, 1982).

The clearest statement by the court with respect to this issue can be found in the decision of the United States Court of Appeals for the Fifth Circuit in the case of *S-1* v. *Turlington*. This case involved the expulsion of nine handicapped students in Florida. The nine plaintiffs in this case were all classified by the school system as "educable mentally retarded" (EMR). Plaintiff's complaint alleged that school officials, by refusing to provide educational services to seven of the nine students expelled, violated their responsibilities under P.L. 94-142 and Section 504. The complaint also alleged that all plaintiffs, including two who had not been expelled, had not received either proper evaluations or individualized educational programs.

The court held that the primary deficit in the school system's expulsion procedure was the failure to determine for each child whether the child's misbehavior was a product of his or her handicapping condition. This individual scrutiny is precisely what the EHA and the implementing regulations are designed to provide and precisely what the expulsion proceeding failed to provide.

The defendants (public school) conceded that students with behavioral problems could not be expelled for conduct related to their handicaps. However, they maintained that since none of the plaintiffs were classified as behavior disordered, their handicaps could not have caused their misbehavior. This position, however, was not supported by court testimony, which supports the view that mental retardation, and other sorts of handicaps, may cause behavioral problems.

Interestingly, plaintiffs argued to the court that under EHA, a handicapped student could never be expelled for misconduct unrelated to his/her handicap. The district court reserved judgment on this issue.

Defendants went on to suggest that the court's order effectively excludes all handicapped children from disciplinary proceedings and creates a "dual system" of discipline for handicapped and non-handicapped students. The court denied that such a system was envisioned. It said that the order merely requires that when a student classified as handicapped engages in misbehavior that, absent the handicap, would result in disciplinary proceedings, the school must first determine whether the child's education program meets his special needs. Further, since EHA requires that the IEP address behavior problems, misconduct may well demonstrate that the initial program was not appropriate for the child.

In summary, it would appear that school districts must explore the possibility that misconduct may be related to a student's handicapping condition prior to use of suspension/expulsion. Further, such a connection is not simply reserved for the emotionally disturbed student and is non-applicable to other handicapping conditions. Finally, the school must explore the possibility that the misconduct is related to an inappropriate placement or program for a handicapped student.

Summary

Suspension/Expulsion procedures have been used for many years by public schools in order to achieve disciplinary control of both handicapped and non-handicapped children and youth. Data of the effectiveness of these procedures is difficult to find, and often these procedures only serve to temporarily remove problems rather than changing behavior.

With the advent of P.L. 94-142 and Section 504, the right to a free, appropriate public education for all handicapped children became law. The use of suspension/expulsion with these students presents numerous problems (previously outlined in this section) since it often abridges access to education.

One possible solution to this problem may be to make better use of IEP teams. For example, the IEP team could rule as a committee on plans for or acts of suspension/expulsion in accordance with state and federal rules and regulations for the handicapped (Barnette & Parker, 1982). Educators and parents working together in the IEP team could consider alternatives available in disciplinary action for the handicapped student and develop an individualized discipline plan. This process could facilitate thoughtful, flexible, and legal planning that would reflect concern for both the needs of the school system as well as the handicapped student.

Finally, even in cases where suspension/expulsion is warranted and used appropriately by school systems, educational services for handicapped students must continue without interruption.

REFERENCES

Barnette, S.M. and Parker, L.G.: Suspension and expulsion of the emotionally handicapped: Issues and practices. Behavior Disorders, 73, 1982. Cambridge, MA: Center for Law and Education, 1982.

Boundy, K.B.: Discipline of handicapped students.

Briefing Paper: Initial Review of Regulations Under Part B of the Education of the Handicapped, as amended. U.S. Department of Education. Washington, D.C., 1981.

Gallup Poll of the public's attitude toward the public schools. *Phi Delta Kappan, September*:37-50, 1982.

Martin, R.: Discipline of Special Education Students, in School Law in Contemporary Society, Topeka, Kansas, National Organization on Legal Problems of Education, 1980.

Pullin, D.: *Disciplinary Exclusion of Handicapped Students*. Cambridge, MA: Center for Law and Education, 1981.

Reutter, E.R., and Hamilton, R.R.: *The Law of Public Education*. New York: The Foundation Press, Inc., 1970.

School Violence Prevention Manual, Technical assistance bulletin No. 12 National School Resource Network. Copyright 1980 Oelgeschlager, Gunn and Hain, Publishers, Inc.

The Education for All Handicapped Children Act, P.L. No. 94-142, 20, U.S.C. 1401 et seq.

The Rehabilitation Act of 1973, P.L. No. 93-112, 29, U.S.C. 794.

Wayson, W.W., and Pinnell, G.S.: Approaches for improving school discipline. Citizens' Guide to Quality Education, Citizens' Council for Ohio Schools, 517 The Arcade, Cleveland, OH 44114, June, 1978.

Blue v. New Haven Board of Education, Civ. No. N81-41 (D. Conn., March 23, 1981).

Board of Education of the City of Peoria v. Illinois State Board of Education 531

F. Supp. 148 (C.D. Ill., 1982).

Campoch:aro v. Califano, Civil Action No. H-78-64 (D. Conn., 1978).

Doe v. Koger, 480 F. Supp. 225 (M.D. Ind., 1979).

Doe v. Maher, No. C-80-4270-MHP (N.D. Cal., December 12, 1980).

Goss v. Lopez, 419 U.S. 565, L. Ed. 725, 95 S. ct. 729 (1975).

Hairston v. Drosick, 423 F. Supp. 180, 183 (S.D. W.Va., 1976).

Howard S. v. Friendswood Independent School District, 454 F. Supp, 634, 641 (S.D. Tex. 1978).

Kaelin v. Grubbs, 682 F.2d 595 (1982).

Lopez v. Salida School District, C.A. No. C-7078 (District Court County of Denver, Colorado, January 20, 1978).

Mattie T. v. Holladay, No. DC 75-31-S (N.D. Miss, July 28, 1977).

Mrs. A.J. v. Special School District No. I, 478 F. Supp. 418 (D. Minn, 1979).

P-1 v. Shedd, C.A. No. 8-78-58, D. Conn. (Consent Decree, March 23, 1979).

Robert M. v. Benton, No. C79-4007 (N.D. Iowa, Western Div., August 13, 1979).

S-1 v. Turlington, No. 79-2742, U.S. Ct. of Appeals, 5th Circuit, 635 F. Supp. 342 (Jan. 26, 1981).

Sherry v. New York State Education Department, 479 F. Supp. 1328 (W.D. N.Y., 1979).

Southeast Warren Community School District v. Department of Public Instruction, No. 231/63181 (Supp. Ct., Iowa, 1979).

Stanley v. School Administrative Unit No. 40, Milford-Mount Vernon, No. 89-9-D, (D.M.H., Jan. 15, 1980).

Stuart v. Nappi, 433 F. Supp. 1235 (D. Conn., 1978).

CHAPTER 6

ADVOCACY IN SPECIAL EDUCATION: PARENTS AS ADVOCATES

THE primary catalyst for change in special education over the last ten years has been the courts. From PARC (1971) through Rowley (1982), lawyers, judges, and legislators rather than educators have shaped the course of education for handicapped children. Today, however, this trend seems to be changing.

Turnbull (1981) cites frequent federal court decisions that indicate that the courts want to avoid the day-to-day management of schools. He suggests that this is not surprising but rather is consistent with the court's view that public schools should essentially be a matter of state and local concern.

Additional support for this premise can be found in the Supreme Court's decision in *Rowley* (1981). The court said that "in assuring that the requirements of the act (P.L. 94-142) have been met, courts must be careful to avoid imposing their view of preferable educational methods upon the state. The primary responsibility for formulating the education to be accorded a handicapped child, and for choosing the educational method most suitable to the child's needs, was left by the act to state and local education agencies in cooperation with the parents or guardian of the child."

The unwillingness of the courts to continue to function as the primary agent in resolving conflicts between schools and parents concerning education of handicapped children is not surprising.

Some reasons for this may include:

1. Constitutionally, education is a state responsibility.
2. The tremendous backlog of court cases could be somewhat alleviated by minimizing special education cases.
3. Decisions about special education for handicapped children should be made by educators, not lawyers and judges
4. The statute (P.L. 94-142) created an administrative remedy for resolving such conflicts: the due process hearing.

If the trend discussed previously continues, the due process hearing, rather than the courts, will become the most significant policy-shaper for the future of special education. Therefore, as the appeals hearing assumes more importance, so also does the parental role in this process.

Parents will need to become effective advocates for their handicapped children. In order to do this, they will need to develop specific skills and strategies pertinent to the hearing process. Specifically, parent training will be necessary. This raises several important questions:

1. What will parent training consist of?
2. Who will provide the training?
3. Who will pay for the costs of such training?
4. What problems already exist in the appeals process that need resolution?

In response to the first question, several authors have provided some useful guidelines. Turnbull (1981) argues that P.L. 94-142 and Section 504 created six standards for the education of handicapped children. The standards are:

1. zero reject
2. non-discriminatory evaluation
3. appropriate education
4. least restrictive placement
5. procedural due process
6. parent participation

These standards would provide a good foundation for any parent training program.

Budoff (1981) has also cited a number of requirements necessary to assist parents in the appeals process. These things include:

1. parent understanding of the law and their rights
2. ability to collect and interpret relevant documents
3. providing testimony at the hearing
4. guarantee of free and easy access to school records
5. access to legal counsel experienced in special education issues
6. funding necessary for independent evaluations and expert witnesses

Other issues parents will need training in include:

1. knowledge of the IEP process
2. knowledge of P.L. 94-142, Section 504 (proposed changes), current important court cases, and pertinent state statutes
3. knowledge of the child's handicapping condition
4. knowledge of curriculum, placement options, and evaluation of student progress

Cutler (1981) lists the following characteristics of an effective advocate:

1. greater concern for the child's best interests than for the concerns or interests of the school system
2. long-term commitment to the child's welfare and to being the child's advocate
3. knowledge of the present needs of the child or the ability to recognize those needs
4. assertiveness in pointing out the child's needs to the people responsible for meeting those needs
5. ability to work with others to develop appropriate and beneficial educational goals and plans for the child
6. ability to find and use information, allies, and resources to put the needed educational plans to work

It may be useful in this process to carefully examine other programs that have trained individuals to function as advocates for the handicapped such as the Surrogate Parent programs required by P.L. 94-142. Specifically, the statute provides that if a child's parent is unknown, unavailable, or if the child is a ward of the state, then the SEA must provide a surrogate parent for that child.

Another view on parent training has been proposed by Simpson (1982). He suggests that parent training should follow the same format as that described by educator training. Specific training should focus on:

1. development of appropriate attitudes
2. specific content training
3. opportunities for parents to express and share feelings and perceptions
4. opportunities to observe acceptable role models
5. simulation activities
6. feedback

He goes on to point out that the curriculum must be fashioned so as to convince parents that only when they are assertive and knowledgeable about the methodology and protocol affecting their children will they be able to adequately assist in serving their children's educational needs.

The question of who should provide the parent training is also significant. The training should not be provided by the SEA or LEA since it would be an apparent conflict of interest. Some options here might be:

1. Creation of an independent agency in each state funded under P.L. 94-142. Perhaps some money set aside for "child find" could be diverted to meet this need.
2. Special interest groups like ARC (Associations for Retarded Citizens), UCP (United Cerebral Palsy), NSAC (National Society for Autistic Children), or CCBD (Council for Children with Behavior Disorders) could meet this need.
3. Attorneys, advocates, professionals, and private school administrators possessing specific skills might donate time to assist in parent training.

Training parents to become effective advocates for their handicapped children will cost money. This money will be needed to develop training materials, to hire competent staff, to provide space in which the training will be held, to rent or buy audiovisual equipment and other necessary materials, and also for other expenses such as phone, postage, and paper.

Several potential sources of funding may exist: first, people may be willing to donate services; second, P.L. 94-142 funds; third, private grants and foundations; fourth, private organizations already committed to the handicapped; and fifth, private industry may donate materials, space, and money.

Some problems inherent in the special education appeals process are already apparent. They can be divided into two general categories (1) those directly related to the appeals process and (2) those related to the politics of special education and human services today.

One problem deals with the cost of the process. Budoff (1981) reported that the hearing process is used disproportionately by upper middle class parents whose children have learning disabilities. He also found that lower class parents did not use the process because of factors such as cost, implicit intimidation of the IEP process, and lack of a parent support system.

Strickland (1982) reported results similar to those found by Budoff. She found that parents who exercise the due process hearing option are usually well educated and in the middle-to-upper socioeconomic levels. She concluded that the overrepresentation of these parents is due to unavailability of time, money, and resources for poor and minority families.

Studies such as these raise serious questions concerning the ability of poor and minority parents to utilize the hearing process. If parents are faced with the decision of feeding, clothing, and caring for their families or paying the costs of a hearing, they will be effectively barred from participating in this process. Some method for assuring that poor and minority families will have access to the process if they want to pursue it will have to be found.

Another problem inherent in the appeals process concerns the status of the relationship between parents and schools during appeals. Stevens (1980) pointed out that rejection of an IEP means taking on the school system. They are risking their relationship with the school and teachers. They feel that rejection of the IEP will result in denial of services, together with rejection of the child and the family by the school system. Parents also fear being intimidated by professionals more knowledgeable in special education jargon than they are.

Stevens (1980) also argues that parents must realize that success in a hearing requires convincing the hearing officer of the child's needs and the educational program required to meet them. Preparation for this process may be especially grueling for parents, who must withstand considerable emotional stress. Parents must also be prepared to bear a financial burden associated with professional witnesses, preparation of evidence, time lost from work, child care, and other services. On the national level, problems related to the economy and the political climate created by the Reagan administration bear on this problem.

Weckstein (1983) suggests that a public funding crisis is now threatening education and other social services. Two causes for the crisis have been proposed: (1) the effects of economic decline, inflation, and unemployment, (2) public funds are further eroded by current government strategies for reversing the economic decline. The resulting decline of resources stemming from these two factors may pit advocates for educational programs against one another, against those who support social services other than education, and against everyone whose income is affected by taxes and inflation.

Some policies currently advocated by the Reagan administration include efforts to deregulate P.L. 94-142 and Section 504, attempts to abolish the Department of Education, block grants which would pit human service agencies against one another in competing for federal funds, and a general devaluation of human services in favor of defense.

In other words, while the need for parental advocacy increases, the political and statutory support is eroding.

Despite problems for parents associated with the hearing process, there may also be advantages. Strickland (1981), who studies parent involvement in the hearing process, reports the following findings:

1. Parents (who participated in hearings) report being treated more as equals than before the hearing.
2. Parents indicate that the hearing provides an education for parents regarding their child's education, structure of the school administration, and the many conflicting interpretations of P.L. 94-142.
3. Pertinent issues are continually brought before the public.
4. Controversial issues are considered with the ultimate potential for clarification of state and federal policy in regard to intended implementation of P.L. 94-142.

SUMMARY

The basic premise of this chapter is that parents will have to play a more active role in advocating for their handicapped children as the involvement of the courts diminishes. Specifically, parents will have to play a more active role in due process hearings; in order to do this effectively, parents will require training. The issue of parent training raises several important questions that must be addressed: First, what will the parents' training consist of? Second, who will provide the training? Third, who will pay for the cost of such training? Fourth, what problems related to parent participation in appeals have been identified and need to be addressed?

Finally, parent training, an issue long neglected in special education, must now be addressed head-on if the gains achieved by and for handicapped children are to be preserved.

REFERENCES

Board of Education of the Hendrick Hudson Central School District v. Rowley, 50 U.S.L.W. 4925.

Budoff, M., and Orenstein, A.: Special education appeals hearings: are they fair and are they helping? *Exceptional Education Quarterly*, 2(2):37-48, 1981.

Cutler, B.: *Unraveling the Special Education Maze*. Champaign, IL: Research Press, 1981.

Pennsylvania Association for Retarded Children v. Pennsylvania, 343 F. Supp, 279 (E.D.Pa. 1972).

Simpson, R.: Future training issues. *Exceptional Education Quarterly*, 3(2):81-88, 1982.

Stevens, M.A.: Appeals—an advocate's view. Appeals News. Massachusetts Department of Education, B.S.E.A, vol. 5, 1980.

Strickland, B.: Parental participation, school accountability, and due process. *Exceptional Education Quarterly*, 3(2):41-49, 1982.

The Education for All Handicapped Children Act, P.L. No. 94-142, 20 U.S.C. 1401 et seq.

The Rehabilitation Act of 1973, P.L. No. 93-112, 29 U.S.C. 794.

Turnbull, H.R.: Legal precedent and the individual case: how much can be generalized from court findings? *Exceptional Education Quarterly*, 2(2):81-90, 1981.

Weckstein, P.: Democratic Economic Development is the Key to Future Quality Education, *Phi Delta Kappan, 64* (6):420-423, 1983.

CHAPTER 7

SELECTED SPECIAL EDUCATION
CASE LAW SUMMARY

S PECIAL education law is constantly in a state of flux. This change may be related to new federal laws or changes in regulations, policy interpretations from the United States Office of Education, or judge-made law.

The purpose of this chapter is to provide the reader with a summary of recent special education cases. These cases must be studied if the reader is to understand what courts are saying in applying federal acts to special education service delivery.

The format of this section is to cluster cases around specific issues. The issues discussed include: clarification of the hearing officer's role, the developmentally disabled act, medical exclusion of handicapped students, extended school year, payment of special education services, IQ tests and handicapped students, handicapped students in private schools, minimum competency testing, damages under P.L. 94-142, optimum vs. adequate placement, procedural safeguards, related services, Section 504 decisions, suspension and expulsion, and who is entitled to receive special education services.

Clarification of the Hearing Officer's Role

Helms v. McDaniel (Georgia, 1982)

ISSUE: Clarification of hearing officers' duties and powers with regard to due process hearings.

CASE: The original case was brought in 1979 after Alice Helms, then nine-years-old, was transferred from a regular class with resource room help to an EMR class, based on an IQ score. The parents fought the placement, deeming it inappropriate.

The case quickly evolved into a case involving the weight that hearing officer decisions have on appeal cases. In Georgia, the hearing officer was treated as a "special master" whose decisions were considered recommendations to state educational officials. The state also contended that it is "fiscally accountable, yet a hearing officer may opt for a more expensive plan for a handicapped child."

The plaintiffs argued that the Georgia system conflicted with the federal law.

DECISION: The Fifth United States Circuit Court of Appeals in its decision stated that Georgia was violating the federal handicapped education law by giving the state board of education the final say in placing handicapped children. Judge Robert Vance said that the state procedure conflicts with federal law "both formally and substantively." The court ruled that because the masters (hearing officers) only make recommendations to the education officials, they do not fulfill the law's requirement for impartial hearing officers who do not work for the education agency.

The case was appealed to the United States Supreme Court, which let the Fifth United States Circuit Court of Appeals' decision stand as it refused to hear the case. By allowing the decision to stand, the court allowed for impartial hearing officers, not state officials, to have the final word on appeals by parents contesting the identification, evaluation, and placement of their handicapped children.

Developmentally Disabled Assistance and Bill of Rights Act

Pennhurst State School v. Halderman (Pennsylvania, 1981)

ISSUE: Does the federal Developmentally Disabled Assistance and Bill of Rights Act require states to assume the cost of providing appropriate treatment in the least restrictive environment for the mentally retarded?

CASE: The United States Supreme Court by a 6–3 margin overturned a Third Circuit Court of Appeals' decision that had held that the Developmentally Disabled Assistance and Bill of Rights Act mandated that states were obligated to provide community living arrangements for residents it determined capable of succeeding in the least restrictive environment. The class action suit initially won both appeals court and trial court rulings that conditions in the Pennhurst State School of Pennsylvania were unsanitary, inhumane, and dangerous.

DECISION: In the Supreme Court majority opinion, Justice William Rehnquist said that the Third United States Court of Appeals read too much into the Developmentally Disabled and Bill of Rights Act. Rehnquist stated, "It establishes a national policy to provide better care and treatment to the retarded and creates funding incentives to induce the states to do so, but the act does no more than that."

The Third Circuit Court of Appeals had ruled that Congress had intended the law to protect the mentally retarded, enacting it under its authority to enforce the Fourteenth Amendment and place conditions on federal funds recipients. Rehnquist countered that Congress would not "implicitly attempt to impose massive financial obligations on states." He went on to write, "We would be attributing far too much to Congress if we held that it required the states at their own expenses to provide certain kinds of treatment. Nothing in the Developmentally Disabled Assistance Act of its stated purpose reveals an intent to require the states to fund new substantive rights." Rehnquist in essence was stating that the act was an encouragement but not a mandate. The court said the disabilities act did not impose obligations that states must meet to receive federal funds. This was an important decision because of the implications that this may have on P.L. 94-142 decisions that may come before the court in future cases.

Exclusion of Handicapped Students for Medical Reasons

Reverend Albert Ely v. Howard County Board of Education (Maryland, 1982)

ISSUE: Can a school district exclude a handicapped student who is a carrier of a contagious disease?

CASE: The Howard County (Maryland) Board of Education decided in November, 1981 to exclude Oliver Ely from its Cedar Lane School for handicapped children because the severely retarded boy was a carrier of hepatitis-B. The teachers of the school district notified the superintendent about the potential problem, and under Maryland law and federal law, school officials can alter a handicapped child's placement if the child is dangerous to himself or others. The school set up home tutoring while the school district looked for a private setting for the child.

Hepatitis-B can be transmitted through saliva and the boy, who functioned at about a 6–8-month mental capacity, constantly drooled, had to be fed, and had a history of biting in the past.

The parents filed a request for a preliminary injunction against the school district with regard to change of placement. The parents had been quite happy with the public school placement and the group home where Oliver lived.

In addition to the problem of placement, the issue of vaccinating the teachers of the school was at odds. A vaccine is supposed to be available in the fall of 1982. As a result, there are the future questions as to whether the school district will pay for the students and teachers to be vaccinated so that Oliver may return to the Cedar Lane program. Finally, one other complicating matter is whether the teachers could be forced into taking a vaccination that they may not wish to take.

DECISION: In the United States District Court's decision, the federal judge ruled that the school district may refuse to admit the boy. The judge in his decision said that while Oliver will suffer because of educational program not being as complete as it previously was, "such hardship and injury which the staff, the other students, and volunteers at Cedar Lane would suffer in the event they contact hepatitis-B is of lesser magnitude." The judge said that he would reconsider the decision in the future if and when a vaccine for hepatitis-B becomes available.

Extended School Year

Georgia Association of Retarded Citizens v. McDaniel (Georgia, 1982)

ISSUE: Do public schools have to provide year-round programs for handicaped students?

CASE: The case was originally filed in 1978 after the Savannah-Chatham School District and the State Board of Education turned down a request from Robert Craine, the named plaintiff, for an education program that would continue into the summer.

According to the plaintiff's attorney, about 350 severely retarded youngsters in the state of Georgia would require year-round schooling. The suit was filed under P.L. 94-142 and Section 504, which guarantee educational rights and prohibit discrimination against handicapped persons.

The state argued that there is no obligation under P.L. 94-142 to provide schooling in excess of 180 days and further stated that none of the plaintiffs in question needed extra schooling. The state provided evidence that one of the plaintiffs regressed in skills but ironically progressed in those life skills taught in school.

DECISION: In a decision that is currently being appealed by both sides, the federal judge stated that the Georgia Public Schools must provide year-round education programs for handicapped students if such programs are necessary for the students' education. The judge declared that the 180-day policy "at best limits individual consideration of the needs of each child . . . and must be discontinued." The ruling closely follows *Armstrong* v. *Kline*, now known as *Battle* v. *Commonwealth*, as the judge indicated, "there can be no question that the defendant must provide schooling in excess for any child that may need it." The judge, much to the chagrin of the plaintiffs, stopped short of ordering extended schooling for the plaintiffs or any other students. Because of the decision, both sides felt that they won and lost and, as a result, both sides were to appeal the case.

Scanlon v. Battle (Pennsylvania, 1982)

ISSUE: Are handicapped children entitled to a school year that they may extend beyond the normal 180 days?

CASE: The case was originally two cases: *Scanlon* v. *Battle* and *Armstrong* v. *Kline*.

The *Armstrong* group argued that the 180-day school-year policy of the state violated the provision of an appropriate education under P.L. 94-142, and the *Scanlon* group did likewise for two handicapped students in that lawsuit. The basis for the lawsuit was that the interruption of services for these youngsters by the traditional summer vacation resulted in a loss of skills for those severely retarded students.

The initial decision in *Armstrong* v. *Kline* came down in 1979 and concluded that the summer recess would in fact interrupt the students' development and preclude the students from achieving self-sufficiency and avoiding institutionalization.

The Commonwealth of Pennsylvania filed an appeal while continuing the summer programs in 1980. In July, 1980, the Third United States Circuit Court of Appeals upheld the United States District Court decision and said that the 180-day rule violated P.L. 94-142 by precluding the proper determination of the content of the required free, appropriate public education.

Pennsylvania fought the Third United States Circuit Court of Appeals' decision, claiming that the education finances and local control would be damaged if the decision were to hold. The National School Board Association, in a friend-of-the-court brief, stated that the precedent decision "affects every school board in the country and could result in a major revision of the very nature of the public education." The Commonwealth of Pennsylvania then appealed to the United States Supreme Court to review the case.

DECISION. On June 22, 1981, the Supreme Court refused to hear the case, letting the Third United States District Court of Appeals' decision stay. Four justices would have been needed to hear the case and only Justice Byron White would have taken the case.

The United States Justice Department asked the Supreme Court not to hear Pennsylvania's claim that it should not have to provide year-round schooling for severely handicapped children. The United States Justice Department claimed that Pennsylvania failed to prove it lacks the money to provide the schooling.

One question regarding the extended school year that was not answered by the courts is, What standard is to be used to determine which students would be eligible?

Financial Disputes Over Who is Responsible for Payment of Special Education Services

Abby Rabinovitz v. New Jersey State Board of Education (New Jersey, 1981)

ISSUE: Does a school system have to pay the cost of a handicapped foster child's placement?

CASE: Abby Rabinovitz is a ten-year-old mentally retarded girl whose biological parents live in New York, while she has lived in a foster home in Hamburg, New Jersey since infancy. According to the plaintiff's attorney, Abby has never gone to school. Abby's biological parents had placed her in the New Jersey home after medical specialists said that she would not do as well in an institution. New York has refused to educate the girl on the ground that it did not place her in the New Jersey foster home. On the other hand, New Jersey has refused to pay her education costs because her biological parents live in New York.

The Hamburg, New Jersey school district is near the New York border. It is a small school district, K–8, with no special education programs. Those students in need of special education are sent to other communities.

The parents went through the New Jersey Board of Education grievance procedure for four years before filing suit in federal district court.

DECISION: United States District Court Judge Lee Sarokin in August, 1981 ordered the Hamburg, New Jersey School District to accept and temporarily pay to educate the child. The judge at that point had not yet set a trial date on whether the Hamburg School District would have to continue to pay the education costs. The judge ordered the parents to post a $10,000 bond to cover interim education costs in case the state of New Jersey wins its claim that it is not responsible. Upon the posting of the bond, the child was to be evaluated and the school system will determine the services that she will be in need of.

Green v. Johnson (Massachusetts, 1979)

ISSUE: Who is responsible for paying for special education services for handicapped youths who are incarcerated and in need of services?

CASE: The suit was brought in 1979 against four Massachusetts county jails that were not providing education for disabled, incarcerated youths. The responsibility for providing special education in jails is a gray area in special education. The state must provide services in state institutions, but the responsibility for county jails is unclear. The relatively short period of time youth offenders spend in jail makes a meaningful education program more difficult.

No one involved in the case disputed the appropriateness of handicapped youth offenders receiving special education services. The state, however, claimed that the responsibility for providing the education services falls on the county, and the counties involved claimed it was the state's obligation.

DECISION: United States District Court Judge Frank Freedman granted a preliminary injunction, ruling that disabled inmates in two county jails must be notified of their rights, referred for evaluation, and provided appropriate services. As part of the injunction, the judge ordered the state to pay for special education services and ordered state and local officials to come up with a plan in thirty days as to who would provide and pay for required services.

IQ Tests and the Placement of Handicapped Students

Parents in Action on Special Education (PASE) v. Hannon (Illinois 1980)

ISSUE: Can IQ tests be used for placing students in classes for educable mentally handicapped?

CASE: In a case involving the desegregation of the Chicago Public Schools, evidence was presented that more than 80 percent of Chicago students in EMR classes are black. Overall, about 66 percent of students in Chicago's special education programs were members of minorities. The plaintiffs charged that "such a condition suggests potential bias in testing, assessment, and placement policies or their implementation. Assessment should not result in disproportionate numbers of minority students being placed in special education classes, where they often continue throughout their school careers." Chicago school officials promised to form a task force to study how phasing out IQ tests would actually be accomplished.

DECISION: United States District Court Judge John Grady ruled that IQ tests were not "culturally unfair or suspect" because Chicago school officials use other criteria that safeguard against racial bias in special education placement.*

Conflict in the Use of Public Money for Handicapped Students Going to Private Schools

Commonwealth of Massachusetts v. Springfield School Committee (Massachusetts, 1981)

ISSUE: Does aid going to private school placements for handicapped children conflict with the laws that do not allow for public aid to private schools?

CASE: The Springfield, Massachusetts School Committee brought suit stating that private school placement for handicapped students was illegal under the state constitution because it amounted to public aid for private schools. The state maintained that the purpose of Chapter 766 was not to give aid to private schools but to provide services that disabled children could not get within the public school. It further stated that Chapter 766 mandates that disabled students be placed in the most appropriate setting, including private schools.

DECISION: The State Supreme Judicial Court ruled in favor of the state. The court applied three standards to untangle the potential conflict in the state laws:

1. Aid going to private schools for the handicapped students was minimal.
2. The money was not going to be used for the purpose of aiding, establishing, or maintaining private schools.
3. The aid did not result in any economic or political abuse.

Minimal Competency Testing and Handicapped Students

Debra B. v. Illinois State Board of Education (Illinois, 1982)

ISSUE: Should handicapped students have to pass minimal competency tests before receiving their high school diplomas?

CASE: A one million dollar lawsuit was filed by fifteen Peoria, Illinois handicapped high school students. The suit claimed that these

---

*This decision was the direct opposite of that in the case of *Larry P.* v. *Riles*. The Chicago School Board, as of July, 1981, voted to stop using IQ tests for placing students in EMH classes despite this previous court decision which is on appeal.

students were illegally denied high school diplomas when they failed a local minimum competency test. The students' attorney said that the test should not be binding on the handicapped students because they did not receive adequate instruction in reading, writing, and math skills. It was also contended by the attorney that the test had not been phased in over a sufficient time period and that it had not been modified for most handicapped students.

The original lawsuit was petitioned to be filed as a class action suit, which was later refused. The plaintiffs sought to prohibit the Illinois State Board of Education from allowing local school districts to develop minimum competency tests. Advocates for handicapped students said MCTs should be based on IEPs and not on the general curriculum. The school district claimed that they were not discriminating by asking all students to come up with certain minimal standards in education. The state school superintendent Donald Gill claimed that the tests are allowed under both P.L. 94-142 and Section 504.

Modifications in the test were refused, although the district was willing to make modifications for the blind and physically handicapped students who would be taking the tests. The school board lawyer also felt that the automatic giving (non-handicapped students who failed) may be a case of reverse discrimination.

DECISION: Despite similar circumstances in the New York case of *Northport–East Northport Union Free School District* v. *Ambach* (New York, 1981), where two handicapped students were allowed to keep their diplomas, United States District Court Judge Robert Morgan wrote, "A local school board requirement for a minimal standard of learning for graduation is completely legitimate, and due process of law does not require pretending that such a standard has been achieved by a person whose handicap clearly makes attainment of that standard impossible or inappropriate."

Morgan went on to comment that to modify the test was "to avoid contact with the mental deficiency (and) would simply be to pretend that the deficiency did not exist. A diploma issued as a result of passing such a modified test would be a perversion of the program."*

---

*In a footnote to this case, the School Code of Illinois was changed to prohibit denial of a diploma if competency test failure is directly related to the student's handicap.

Debra P. v. Turlington (Florida, 1981)

ISSUE: Can school officials deny diplomas to students on the basis of failure of the state's minimal competency test?

CASE: In 1978, Florida school districts were ordered to establish graduation standards beginning with that school year based in part on a functional literacy test. Students who completed all requirements except for passing the test were awarded certificates of completion rather than diplomas.

In the case of *Debra P.* v. *Turlington*, the plaintiffs charged that the state had not proven that the test reflects what is taught in school. The attorney for the black student plaintiffs claimed that the basic skills test punished black students for deficiencies created by the dual education system in effect from 1890-1967. This was in violation of the Fourteenth Amendment.

The state maintains it can prove that the test material is taught in the Florida schools. In addition, the state plans to use the test as a graduation requirement by the 1982-83 school year, and by that time none of the students in the state would have attended a segregated school.

DECISION: The Fifth United States Circuit Court of Appeals ruled that the Florida schools cannot deny diplomas to students who fail the state's basic skills test until the state proves the test reflects what is taught in school. The three-judge appeals panel stated that the "overriding legal issue of the appeal is whether the state of Florida can constitutionally deprive public school students of their high school diplomas on the basis of an examination which may cover matter not taught through the curriculum." The appeals court remanded the case to the United States District Court for the Middle District of Florida.

Northport–East Northport Union Free School District v. Ambach (New York, 1981)

ISSUE: Can handicapped students keep their high school diplomas even though they failed the state's minimal competency test?

CASE: Two handicapped high school students, one who is neurologically impaired and the other classified as trainable mentally retarded, were given high school diplomas by their school district despite the fact that they failed the required state minimal competency exam. Under New York state policy, handicapped students who meet their IEP goals are eligible to receive certificates instead of diplomas. The Northport–East Northport School District's policy differed. It was their policy to award diplomas to handicapped students based on satisfactory completion of IEP objectives. The state education commissioner ordered the diplomas revoked, thus prompting the lawsuit.

DECISION: The New York State Supreme Court ruled that the two handicapped students may keep their high school diplomas even though they failed the state's minimal competency test. This was considered the first lawsuit brought to test the validity of standardized competency tests of minimal competency for handicapped children. Instead, the judge said the students' rights under the Fourteenth Amendment with regard to due process were violated because they did not have adequate notice of the state's new graduation requirements. The judge felt that the students should have been notified in the elementary school; that would have been impossible because of the only recent trend toward minimal competency testing. The judge did not rule on the violations with regard to P.L. 94-142 or Section 504 but solely on the Fourteenth Amendment, stating that the students "had a legitimate expectation of the receipt of the diplomas. Therefore the diploma represents a property interest for the purposes of due process."*

Monetary Damages Under P.L. 94-142

Anderson v. Thompson (Wisconsin, 1981)

ISSUE: Are monetary damages available under P.L. 94-142?

CASE: Wisconsin's education department found that Monica Anderson was not emotionally disturbed and recommended that she be placed in a program for the educable mentally retarded. The parents disagreed and sent her to a private school instead. The trial court ruled that the state recommendation of an EMR class was inappropriate, but said the parents could not collect damages under P.L. 94-142. The parents appealed the case to the Seventh United States Circuit Court of Appeals under a 1971 civil rights act that would allow federal civil rights damages to be sought whenever individuals are denied the benefits of a federal law.

---

*The state plans to appeal.

DECISION: Judge Luther Swygert in his decision stated that parents were not entitled to damages under P.L. 94-142. He went on to state that award damages for the improper placement would be under "exceptional circumstances only." There are, according to the decision, only two exceptional circumstances in which limited damages might be awarded: (1) when a placement endangers a child's physical health, and (2) when a placement is made in "a egregious fashion" in violation of the law's placement procedures. According to the judge, P.L. 94-142 intended no damages for an "incorrect program decision." The judge further stated that he would dismiss damages under the 1971 civil rights act and that P.L. 94-142 had exclusive remedies built in, with its private right of action and its elaborate administrative enforcement system. Therefore, according to the decision, the old civil rights law would not apply because it dealt with "no exclusive remedy for violations."

Jaworski v. Rhode Island Board of Regents (Rhode Island, 1982)

ISSUE: Are damages available to plaintiffs under P.L. 94-142?

CASE: James Jaworski entered the Pawtucket, Rhode Island school system in 1967 and experienced considerable difficulty in the basics of education, including reading, writing, and arithmetic. It was not until December, 1973 that he was diagnosed as dyslexic and placed in a private school. The school system refused to pay the tuition because it had a program for dyslexic children. The Jaworski's appealed through administrative and court channels seeking reimbursement for tuition paid at the private school that the boy was enrolled in. They had originally asked the court to force the school system to place their son in the private school. By the time the case reached the Rhode Island District Court, Jaworski had graduated from high school and only payment damages were left for the court to decide.

DECISION: In the United States District Court decision, the judge wrote that P.L. 94-142 "is concerned with establishing procedural safeguards for ensuring the proper placement of handicapped children." In his ruling, Chief Judge Raymond Pettine refused to reimburse the Jaworski's, stating under P.L. 94-142 "that a damages remedy was not generally intended."

Optimum v. Adequate Placement

Bales v. Clark (Virginia, 1981)

ISSUE: Does a school system have to provide an ideal education to handicapped students under the law (P.L. 94-142)?

CASE: Evelyn Bales was a thirteen-year-old girl who received severe head injuries in an automobile accident in 1977. She is now required to receive academic tutoring and extensive speech and language therapy. She had attended the Home for Crippled Children in Pittsburgh for two years of rehabilitation after the accident when her parents decided that she should attend a private school in Virginia for handicapped children. The school recommended that she be placed in a public education center closer to her home school district. Evelyn attended the center for two years, although her parents never signed the IEP.

The Bales went through appeal procedures and then to federal court in an attempt to have the child educated in the private school.

DECISION: Federal District Court Judge Dortsch Warriner stated that a handicapped child is not entitled to an "ideal" education under the law but simply one that is "appropriate." "An appropriate education is not synonymous with the best possible education." The judge further stated, "neither they (Bales) nor any other parents have the right under the law to write a prescription for an ideal education for their child and have the prescription filled at public expense. The law requires an appropriate public education. Efforts to build this requirement into something more will threaten the substantial gains already made in the education of the handicapped." The judge wrote, "no language in state or federal law can properly be read as mandating that costs may not be considered in determining what education is appropriate for a handicapped child." He said such factors as the difference in travel costs to the two schools "must be considered in determining the appropriateness of the schools." The parents had also requested reimbursement for summer tutoring that they had obtained for their daughter. According to the judge, "The child is not entitled to a year-round schooling without showing an irreparable loss of progress during summer months." No loss was shown.

Springdale v. Grace (Arkansas, 1981)

ISSUE: Is a child who is handicapped entitled to an "ideal" education under the law (P.L. 94-142)?

CASE: Sherry Grace is a deaf fourth-grade student. She was either born deaf or lost her hearing before she developed speech. Sherry entered the State School for the Deaf in Little Rock, Arkansas at age six and at the time was functioning as a child of two years. She developed her reading and math abilities to the mid-second-grade level over the next three calendar years. The Grace family then moved to the Springdale, Arkansas School District in the northwestern part of the state and there sought a certified teacher of the deaf to teach Sherry in the Springdale system.

The school district claimed the only appropriate place for the girl at that point in her life was the state school. This meant that the girl would have to move back to Little Rock and live at the state school to attend it. The parents argued, "The school district has no right to dictate where she'll live." The parents wanted her to grow up in the community with their family and not be segregated. The school district countered that the one-to-one program they had to offer doesn't meet the "mainstreaming" requirements of P.L. 94-142 and was not the "most" appropriate schooling.

DECISION: The Eighth United States Circuit Court of Appeals upheld a federal district court decision that the Springdale School District could provide Sherry Grace with the appropriate education required by P.L. 94-142 even though it believed that the youngster would get better treatment at the State School for the Deaf in Little Rock.

The court stated in its decision in upholding the lower court's decision, "The fact that Sherry may not, like many non-handicapped children, reach her full potential is not due to any error in the district court's interpretation of the act of its finding that the Springdale School District could appropriately educate Sherry, but instead from forces outside the school environment. The act (P.L. 94-142) cannot remedy a child's cultural and sociological environment nor force parents by threatening to remove the child from the home to become partners with the state in insuring that a child reach her full potential."

Procedural Safeguards Under P.L. 94-142

Foster v. District of Columbia Board of Education (District of Columbia, 1982)

ISSUE: Do parents have the right to place their handicapped child in a private school at public cost when a school district unduly delays placing a child?

CASE: Jean Foster, the mother of an emotionally disturbed teenage girl with learning disabilities, filed suit against the District of Columbia Board of Education claiming that the school district delayed too long in providing the special education services that the girl, Cassandra Foster, was entitled to. The school district denied the charges.

DECISION: In the United States District Court decision, the court came down on the side of the plaintiff. The judge ordered the school district to pay for the placement because it delayed so long in considering the child's case. The judge wrote "that the delay shows a disregard for her welfare." He further stated that school officials "shirked their responsibility to provide for publicly supported special education to which Cassandra Foster was entitled."

Gregg B. v. Board of Education of Lawrence School District (New York, 1982)

ISSUE: Do parents have the right to place their handicapped child in a private setting at public cost when a school district unduly delays placing the child?

CASE: The Lawrence School District did not tell the parents of Gregg B., an emotionally disturbed teenager, that his placement in Pennsylvania's Mill Creek School during the 1979-80 school year could not be paid for by the school district because the school was not approved by the state education department according to court document.

DECISION: United States District Court Judge Eugene Nickerson wrote in his decision favoring the plaintiffs that "such awards are consistent with the goals of P.L. 94-142 by obliging school boards to pay for their failure to make timely placement decisions."

Davis v. Maine Endwell Central School District (New York, 1981)

ISSUE: Do all administrative procedures in obtaining special education services have to be exhausted before federal courts will intervene?

CASE: Norman Davis claimed that his thirteen-year-old learning disabled son, James, was excluded from his elementary classroom because of his handicap.

The school district arranged for home teaching of one hour per day pending the evaluation of the child. The school decided that evaluations determined that the child would best be served in a residential school. Davis sued the school district after the IEP committee had scheduled a meeting to discuss the matter with him.

Davis wished to skip over the procedural steps spelled out in the P.L. 94-142 regulations. He stated that if "claims are relegated to the Education for All Handicapped Children Act, procedures, the rules of evidence, burden of proof and degree of deference to agency expertise could combine to defeat legitimate claims of discrimination."

DECISION: The Federal District Court of New York and the Second United States Circuit Court of Appeals ruled that all administrative procedures challenging special education placement must first be exhausted before federal courts may intervene. The district judge ruled that the judicial intervention in cases before the P.L. 94-142 appeal process "would serve to frustrate legislative intent." The court found that Davis had totally sidestepped the administrative appeal process and noted the court's lack of specialized knowledge in making educational decisions.

Stemple v. Board of Education (Maryland, 1981)

ISSUE: Can parents remove a child from a special education placement while a dispute over the program's adequacy exists?

DECISION: The United States Supreme Court upheld a Fourth United States Circuit Court of Appeals ruling that parents who withdraw their child from an objectionable special education program lose their right to recover private school tuition costs. The lower court had ruled that the parents had a duty to keep their child in a class until a dispute over the program's adequacy was settled.

Concerned Parents v. New York City Board of Education (New York, 1981)

ISSUE: Due process in the transferring of handicapped students.

CASE: Harlem parents claimed that the New York City Board of Education jeopardized the rights of their handicapped children under P.L. 94-142. The school board in fall of 1979 transferred 185 students from Harlem in what parents described as a "poorly planned and disconcerting move." The school board claimed that the move was a budgetary one and would not affect the students' education because they would be continuing in a program that was the same as the one they were leaving.

DECISION: The Second United States District Court of Appeals ruled that prior notice and hearing requirements under P.L. 94-142 were not violated. The court stated that "the school board's budget-minded transfer placed the handicapped students in the same classification, the same school district, and the same type of educational program special classes in regular schools."

Further action on the appeal by parents was halted at the United States Supreme Court, as the high court let the lower court's decision stay by refusing to hear the appeal.

Youngberg v. Romeo (Pennsylvania, 1981)

ISSUE: Does shackling and other restrictive measures violate the mentally retarded under the Due Process Clause of the Fourteenth Amendment?

CASE: The case involves Nicholas Romeo, a resident of Pennhurst State School, Pennsylvania. In this case, the state school claimed that restraints were necessary to keep Nicholas Romeo from hurting himself and others. They maintained that only deliberate neglect constituted a violation of a patient's right to treatment. The plaintiffs claimed that shackling and other restrictive measures were a violation of the constitutional right to least restrictive treatment.

DECISION: The Third United States District Court ruled that Romeo had a right to the least restrictive treatment and the officials operating Pennsylvania's Pennhurst State School had violated that right. This is one of several cases involving the deinstitutionalizing of the Pennhurst State School.*

---

*The case was appealed by the defendants to the United States Supreme Court.

Related Services under P.L. 94-142

Tatro v. Texas (Texas, 1980)

ISSUE: Related services under P.L. 94-142. Do school districts have to provide catheterization as a related service for handicapped children?

CASE: Amber Tatro is a six-year-old girl who is partially paralyzed because of a congenital spinal disorder. The parents of the girl filed suit against the Irving Unified School District after the district refused to pay the costs of the catheterization. The parents claimed that catheterization is a related service under P.L. 94-142 and would allow Amber to remain in the least restrictive environment (in this case, the regular classroom setting). Amber had been attending a private school since the original suit was filed in October, 1979.

DECISION: In what is considered a landmark decision to date, the United States Fifth Circuit Court in September, 1980 ruled that catheterization is a support service required under the law to help handicapped students benefit from special education. The Fifth United States Circuit Court of Appeals upheld that decision in May, 1981. The court ruled that under P.L. 94-142, Amber is entitled to have her IEP modified to have the school district furnish catheterization for the girl to stay in a regular classroom. Without a change in the IEP, Amber's education program failed to provide a related service that is required to assist her to benefit from special education, the court said. Judge Patrick Higginbotham stated in his decision that, "Amber will suffer irreparable harm if the catheterization services are not provided in school." He also found that the cost to the school district (estimated at $40 per day) is minimal "and that the public interest is served by ensuring that Amber receives a free, appropriate public education."*

Scanlon v. Tokarcik (Pennsylvania, 1981)

ISSUE: Are schools required under the "related services" section

---

*Largely because of this case, the Carter administration in its last days in January, 1981 ruled in a Department of Education policy statement that catheterization is a related service under P.L. 94-142 and required under Section 504 as well. The Department of Education also said that school districts were not required to pay for or provide other medical services needed for catheterization. The Reagan administration has not finalized its policy.

of P.L. 94-142 to provide catheterization for handicapped students?

CASE: Amber Tokarcik is a fourth-grade student in the Forest Hills, Pennsylvania School District. She has spina bifida and is paralyzed from the waist down. Amber in in a wheelchair, has no mental deficiencies, and is in a regular classroom. She needs catheterization every four hours because she cannot empty her bladder without help. The lawsuit brought by her parents was under P.L. 94-142 and Section 504.

The Commonwealth of Pennsylvania claimed that the girl is not mentally handicapped and is in a regular classroom and therefore is not entitled to receive related services. The Commonwealth of Pennsylvania and in a friend-of-the-court brief by the Pennsylvania School Boards Association claimed that the family should be responsible for the catheterization because it is in fact a medical service, which is not required by law. The law does require school health services, but catheterization goes beyond that because it must be ordered by a doctor, claimed the defendants. Pennsylvania drew the catheterization situation to being similar to such services as injections, blood transfusions, or kidney dialysis. According to Pennsylvania, if schools were required to provide such services, they would end up doing so "regardless of whether that child is in need of or is receiving any special education."

DECISION: The Third United States Circuit Court of Appeals said that while catheterization is not mentioned in P.L. 94-142, it is clearly a "related service" required by the law to help handicapped children. The court based its decision largely on the landmark *Tatro* v. *State of Texas* case that had earlier ruled that catheterization is a support service required under the law to help handicapped children benefit from special education. Although schools are not required under the act to provide students with medical services, the school must provide catheterization because P.L. 94-142 regulations included services provided by a qualified school nurse, according to the decision. The court stated that the catheterization could in fact be performed by a school nurse.*

Kruelle v. Biggs (Delaware, 1981)

ISSUE: Do schools have to provide for residential care when the

---

*A possible appeal by the Commonwealth of Pennsylvania is pending.

needs of the student are not entirely educational?

CASE: Paul Kruelle is a severely retarded boy with emotional problems. It was stated that the then thirteen-year-old needed the special services that a residential program could provide. The main issue was whether the placement would be for educational rather than emotional, social, or medical reasons. The stated conceded that the boy might need attention beyond the normal school day. They argued, however, that the boy's needs go beyond education-related services and therefore they were not obligated to provide for them. Their contention was that P.L. 94-142 limits how much responsibility can be imposed on education officials for the health care of children.

DECISION: In a Third United States Circuit Court of Appeals decision, the court ruled that the severely retarded-emotionally disturbed boy needs to be placed in a residential facility and SEA and LEA officials are obliged to provide the services. The court stated that P.L. 94-142 specifically assigned responsibility of handicapped children to schools.

In the Interest of Claudia K. (Illinois, 1981)

ISSUE: Do school districts have to bear the costs of psychotherapy for a suicidal student who is a ward of the court but not a student in the public schools?

CASE: Claudia Knudton at the time of the case was an eighteen-year-old who had what was described as a "life-threatening suicidal condition." The costs of her psychotherapy at the time of the case were $38,000 and going up. Claudia had been in a residential placement until the summer of 1981 when school officials at Wauconda, Illinois sought to refer her to a state mental health program from which she would have been barred when she turned eighteen in October, 1981. Suit was filed on behalf of the student, claiming that Claudia had a right to a free and appropriate education, and, at the same time, damages were filed for reimbursement by the school district for the hospital and doctor care that Claudia had received up until that point. The local school board and the Illinois State Board of Education interpreted its state handicapped law, under which the suit was filed, as separating the costs of education from those of psychotherapy, and that school districts only had to pay for placement and educational expenses.

DECISION: In November, 1981, Illinois Circuit Court Judge Bernard Drew ordered the school districts to pay for Claudia Knudton's psychotherapy and residential placement. The judge ruled on the case just before Claudia turned eighteen years of age and, by imposing an Illinois law affecting juveniles, ruled it as an emergency order. By doing this, the judge bypassed the administrative hearing process called for in the handicapped law.*

Relevant 504 Decisions

Jane Doe v. New York University (New York, 1981)

ISSUE: Does a university have to readmit a medical student who voluntarily left school because of mental illness?

CASE: A student known as Jane Doe had filed suit under Section 504 of the Rehabilitation Act of 1973 claiming that New York University discriminated against her because of previous mental illness problems, and that she was otherwise qualified to enter that University's medical school.

Jane Doe had a psychiatric history of self-destructive behavior. Doe claimed that she had undergone therapeutic treatment and her most recent psychiatric problems were in 1977. Since that time, Doe had worked at various stressful jobs. Among them were a position at the then HEW and an earned master's degree from Harvard University's School of Public Health. While working at HEW, the Office of Civil Rights found that violations of Section 504 had occurred against Jane Doe in her attempt at readmission.

New York University felt that students with a mental illness history were required to prove there is no risk of recurring harmful behavior. New York University contended that school officials using proper medical tests should be the final judge of when a student is qualified for admission.

DECISION: In an early court order, New York University was found to have violated Section 504 and ordered to readmit Jane Doe. The Second United States Circuit Court of Appeals overturned the lower court's decision. It stated that Jane Doe did not have to be readmitted to New York University because there was

---

*The case was supposed to be heard by the Illinois Supreme Court on an emergency appeal by the school district.

substantial risk that her past "self-destructive and antisocial conduct" would crop up again. In addition to the final verdict, Appeals Judge Gerard Goettel gave no weight to the earlier finding of Section 504 violation by the Office of Civil Rights. The judge claimed that the OCR was biased in favor of Jane Doe and he criticized that department's procedures and personnel. Earlier, the judge had blasted Congress for "social engineering" by passing Section 504.

Doe v. Syracuse School District (New York, 1981)

ISSUE: Can an employer make pre-employment inquiries about mental illness?

CASE: An unnamed teacher applicant charged that he was denied a position in the Syracuse School District after he acknowledged having been mentally ill seven years previously while in the United States Air Force. A school physician found him to be physically and mentally qualified for the position he sought.

The school district maintained that the applicant was not hired because there were no openings in his field. The question of whether the illegal inquiry was the main reason for rejection was the issue that was going to trial.

The applicant filed suit under Section 504 indicating any history of mental illness and treatment that would bar him from employment that he was otherwise qualified for was a direct violation of the statute.

DECISION: The United States District Court judge ruled in favor of the plaintiff. Judge Howard Munson indicated that the "vital statistics form on the application was in violation of Section 504. The judge noted that the HEW secretary in 1977 concluded that, "a general prohibition of pre-employment inquiries was the most appropriate method for implementing Section 504."

Further action was delayed and would take the form of a trial as to whether the Syracuse School District did in fact not hire that applicant because of his answer to the mental health question.

Schornstein v. The New Jersey Division of Vocational Rehabilitation Services (New Jersey, 1981)

ISSUE: Does a state under Section 504 of the Rehabilitation Act of 1973 have to provide an interpreter for a deaf college student?

CASE: The State of New Jersey was sued by Ruth Ann Schornstein, a deaf student in attendance at Kean College, in August, 1980 when the public schools and the state rehabilitation agency refused to pay for her sign-language interpreter. The rehabilitation agency was paying for her books and tuition, but claimed that it was the state college's (Kean) responsibility to pay for the interpreter. The college refused to pay.

The attorney general argued that neither the college nor the agency did in fact have to pay. The college's responsibility was under Section 504 of the Rehabilitation Act of 1973, which bars discrimination against otherwise qualified handicapped individuals. The state rehabilitation agency's responsibility was under Title I, which regulates how federal matching funds will be administered according to the state attorney general.

DECISION: The federal district court decided in favor of Ms. Schornstein. In its decision, the court said that the state's blanket refusal to provide interpreters to students was a direct violation of the federal law under which the state accepted matching funds to run vocational rehabilitation programs.

Judge Herbert Stern ruled that because the New Jersey Division of Vocational Rehabilitation Services had accepted Ms. Schornstein as a client and agreed to pay her educational expenses, it could not refuse to pay for essential services necessary to overcome her handicap. This was an interpretation of the Title I section, the judge said. The judge did not go into the college's responsibility under Section 504.

Pushkin v. Regents of the University of Colorado (Colorado, 1981)

ISSUE: Can a college student be barred from a graduate psychiatry program because he is physically handicapped?

CASE: Doctor Joshua Pushkin filed charges against the University of Colorado under Section 504 of the Rehabilitation Act of 1973 claiming the school discriminated against him and that he was an otherwise qualified handicapped individual. The University of Colorado program received federal aid.

The University of Colorado claimed that Pushkin was unqualified because he was unable to deal emotionally with potential patient responses to his handicap, a prerequisite for an effective psychiatrist. This was based on a rating by psychiatrists who interviewed him.

Pushkin introduced evidence of other psychiatrists saying that he was fully capable of empathizing with patients and dealing with their emotional reactions.

Unlike the *Southeastern Community College* v. *Davis* decision, the University of Colorado did not contend that substantial program modification would have to be made for Joshua Pushkin or that his disability was so great as to preclude him from practicing psychiatry.

DECISION: The University of Colorado was ordered to admit Doctor Joshua Pushkin to its psychiatric residency program in a federal district court decision. The judge ruled that Doctor Pushkin was denied admission based solely on his handicap. The judge in his decision stated that Pushkin was qualified emotionally and his rejection was caused by the bias of interviewers.

Suspension and Expulsion of Handicapped Students Under P.L. 94-142

S-1 v. Turlington (Florida, 1981)

ISSUE: Can a handicapped student be expelled from school?

CASE: The case was initially filed in 1979 after the Hendry County School Board of Florida had expelled seven educable mentally retarded students in 1977 and 1978 for misconduct, including sexual acts against other students, masturbation, defiance of authority, and vandalism. The students won a 1979 preliminary injunction against the school board dealing with the expulsion only. A trial still remains to be held on the issue of $7.5 million in damages claimed against the school board.

The Florida schools argued that P.L. 94-142 was not intended to create a dual discipline system based on whether a child is handicapped or not. The schools' attorney claimed that Congress, in enacting P.L. 94-142, "had (not) intended to do away with such a time-honored discipline tool." The state argued that if handicapped students were dealt with differently on discipline matters, it would only be a matter of time before a handicapped and non-handicapped student was expelled while the handicapped student continued to receive services.

The preliminary injunction of 1979 was upheld on January 26, 1981 by the Fifth United States Circuit Court of Appeals. Judge

Joseph Hatchett, representing a three-judge panel, said expulsion is "a proper disciplinary tool under the federal handicapped education and anti-discrimination laws, but a complete cessation of educational services is not." The decision went on to say, "before a handicapped student can be expelled, a trained knowledgeable group of persons must determine whether the student's misconduct bears a relationship to his handicapping condition."

According to the three-judge panel, expulsion must be accompanied by a determination of whether the handicapped student's misconduct is related to his handicap. Public Law 94-142 prohibits exclusion from a federally funded program because of an individual's handicap. The court stated that the Florida schools "made no such determination."

In summation, the Fifth United States Circuit Court of Appeals said "that expulsion is a change in placement for handicapped students and schools must follow procedures under federal handicapped education law (P.L. 94-142) before taking such action."

DECISION: The United States Supreme Court refused to review the Fifth United States Circuit Court of Appeals ruling in November, 1981.*

Board of Education of the City of Peoria District 150 v. Illinois State Board of Education (Illinois, 1982)

ISSUE: Can schools suspend handicapped students for short periods of time without first deciding if the offense is due to their disability or to an improper education placement?

CASE: The original case involves the Peoria School District's suspension of a learning disabled seventeen-year-old student, David Buckley, after the student swore at a teacher who kept him after school for disrupting a class.

Buckley's parents charged that the suspension was a change in placement under P.L. 94-142. The parents demanded a hearing, as allowed under P.L. 94-142, and wanted all mention of the suspension removed from their son's permanent record. The hearing officer gave approval to the suspension and refused to clear the record, stating that the outburst was not perpetrated by the handicap. Illi-

---

*This case may reach the Supreme Court at a later date because the full trial and damages being sought is still in the lower courts.

nois State Education Superintendent, Donald Gill, reversed the hearing officer's decision.

The Peoria School District, in turn, sued the Illinois State Board of Education stating that a student such as Buckley with a "slight" disability should be treated the same as a "regular" student. The state contended, however, that, "The emphasis of the handicapped act is in individual determinations. There are children out there who need continuous service due to the severity or nature of their handicap. There are other students who probably would suffer no harm." According to the state, Peoria never determined where David Buckley fell.

DECISION: The judge, Robert Morgan, decided in Peoria's favor, stating, "Such a brief period of enforced absence, possibly equivalent to that often caused by a common cold, simply cannot reasonably be described as a change in a handicapped child's placement or termination of educational services." The judge added that "there is absolutely no social or other value in assuming that the child's outburst in these circumstances was due to inadequate placement." In summation, the judge stated, "any theory that some harm of the brief interruption of classroom work could outweigh the educational value of the suspension here can only be recognized as pure imagination or a feeble attempt at rationalization of a preconceived notion that handicapped students whatever the handicap are free of classroom discipline."

Reineman v. Valley View Community School District #365 (Illinois, 1981)

ISSUE: Can a handicapped student be repeatedly suspended even though he is considered handicapped?

CASE: William Reineman, seventeen-years-old, had a history of some thirty suspensions from the Valley View Community School District. Following a November, 1980 suspension, the parents filed suit. They charged that from at least March, 1979, the school district should have known that their son was handicapped. According to the school district, the boy was not evaluated until May, 1980 and not classified as learning disabled until January, 1981. The parents sued under P.L. 94-142 and Section 504 claiming that the repeat suspensions were a change in educational placement and that the school district was nearly two years tardy in evaluating and placing the boy.

DECISION: In the November, 1981 decision, a United States District Court dismissed the parents' claims regarding the change of placement and the tardiness in evaluation and placement of William Reineman. An appeal to the Seventh United States Circuit Court of Appeals was filed.

Who is Entitled to Receive Special Needs Services?

New Jersey Association of Retarded Citizens v. Department of Human Services (New Jersey, 1982)

ISSUE: Do state institutions have to provide an education for the severely retarded?

CASE: The lawsuit was originally filed in 1977 before the enactment of P.L. 94-142 took effect. The original complaint stated that "education" for the severely retarded was designed "to make people more malleable members of the institution." Since the original suit, New Jersey has upgraded its program and is now monitored by the courts.

DECISION: The New Jersey State Supreme Court ruled that New Jersey must provide mentally retarded children in state institutions at least four hours a day of instruction in the least restrictive environment. The only justification for less instruction, the court declared, would be "the compelling medical circumstances" of a child exhausted by a four-hour program. "But our (court) view is that there is no other excuse."

Akers v. Bolton (Kansas, 1982)

ISSUE: Should all children found to have epilepsy receive special education and/or related services?

CASE: Plaintiff Anthony Akers (presently nineteen-years-old) suffered from seizures since the age of ten and was put on anticonvulsive drugs while a student in the Unified School District in Wichita, Kansas. He was not diagnosed as epileptic until five years after the initial seizures. At that time, he had been suspended from school because of run-ins with teachers and students that sometimes led to seizures. Akers reentered school in 1979 and was refused special education despite repeated requests to the schools by the boy's mother.

Coplaintiff Phillip Moore (sixteen-years-old) was diagnosed as epileptic in 1978 and placed on anti-convulsant medication. The medicine, however, contributed to violent rages that led Moore to leave school for two months. When he returned, he "was ridiculed by some of his classmates and dropped one class in which ridicule had been particularly acute." Moore left school again. The next fall, after the Moores joined the Akers in the lawsuit, he was evaluated for special education services. His plan, which satisfied his family, consisted mainly of monitoring his classroom performance and counseling.

DECISION: In a United States District Court decision, Judge Patrick Kelly ruled in favor of the Unified School District of Wichita, stating, "that identification of epileptic children who do not need special education might result in the unnecessary stigmatization of those children, and that this problem might be compounded by the inevitable misdiagnosis of some children." The judge went on to say, "it is undisputed that not all epileptic children are in need of special education or related services. The special rights under the statute (P.L. 94-142) do not run to all epileptic children as a class."

The decision was the first nationwide on the subject and was based on a factual issue leaving no grounds for an appeal according to the parents' attorney.

Thiessen v. Sanders (Nevada, 1982)

ISSUE: Are mentally retarded children under the age of three entitled to an education paid for by the state when other handicapping conditions are allowed such services?

CASE: This case was presented in the Nevada state courts. Parents of three mentally retarded children filed suit in the Nevada state courts under Section 504 of the Rehabilitation Act of 1973. The plaintiffs claimed that, "Since 1905, without exception, the blind and deaf have been eligible for support, education, and care at any age" under a Nevada law. The parents also stated that there is "no rational basis" for giving priority to the deaf and blind. The Nevada law does not admit non-handicapped students to school before the age of six, but educates mentally retarded children from age three and deaf and blind children from birth. The parents claimed that the law violates their children's Fourteenth Amendment equal protection rights as well as being discriminatory, which is in violation of Section 504.

The state claims that such an argument would require educating all children, handicapped or not, beginning at birth simply because the deaf and blind may be served at that age. The state claims that their concern is not a fiscal one but a question of responsibility and authority.

DECISION: In a decision by Nevada's First Judicial Court, it was stated that giving priority to the deaf and blind does not violate other children's equal protection rights. The court found that the Nevada law does not violate Section 504, because Section 504 allows recipients of federal funds to offer services or benefits exclusively to handicapped persons or certain classes of handicapped persons. It further found that the state law did not violate P.L. 94-142 because that law did not require education of handicapped children before the age of three.*

---

*The decision has been appealed to the Nevada Supreme Court by the plaintiffs.